THE
U-2
AFFAIR

THE U-2 AFFAIR

★

DAVID WISE

and

THOMAS B. ROSS

★

LONDON

THE CRESSET PRESS

First published in Great Britain in 1963,
by The Cresset Press, 11 *Fitzroy Square, London, W.*1

Printed in Great Britain by Lowe & Brydone (Printers) Ltd.
*London, N.W.*10

Contents

Illustrations

Between pages 134 and 135

THE
U-2
AFFAIR

The Bridge

AT DAWN IN BERLIN, THE DARK-green superstructure of the Glienicker Bridge emerged faintly through the mists clinging to the Havel River.

It was an ugly, swaybacked span, named the "Bridge of Unity" to commemorate the alliance of the United States and the Soviet Union in World War II. At its center was a six-inch white line. On one side was West Berlin, on the other, East Germany.

"Sie Verlassen Den Amerikanischen Sektor" the sign on the western side warned, in German, Russian, and English: "You Are Leaving the American Sector."

The morning was cloudy and chill. A few fishermen lounged on the banks of the river. East German police in mustard-colored uniforms stood guard on their side with tommy guns. West German police patrolled the other.

Shortly after 8:00 A.M. on the tenth of February, 1962, two black German compact cars arrived quietly on the American side. A few minutes later three black Soviet Zil limousines pulled up on the East German side.

At 8:20 A.M. three Americans cautiously walked out toward the white line. One was James Donovan, a short, silver-haired New York attorney, ex-counsel to the Office of Strategic Services.[1] Another was Allan Lightner, assistant chief of the United States Mission in West Berlin. The third was a faceless agent of the Central Intelligence Agency.

On the East German side, three Soviet officials were waiting at the center of the bridge. Their leader was Ivan A. Shishkin, second secretary of the Soviet Embassy in East Berlin. One of the others was an agent of the K.G.B., the Soviet Secret Police.

Across the white line, five yards behind the three Americans, stood a slight, balding man with dark glasses and a thin, ascetic face. He was the chief Russian espionage agent for the North American continent until his capture in 1957 in a Manhattan hotel. Much like any traveler, he had a canvas suitcase with him on the bridge.

He was manacled to a high official of the United States Department of Justice. His name was Rudolf Ivanovich Abel.

Five yards behind the three Russians a husky, dark-haired American waited in a fur cap and a heavy overcoat. He, too, had luggage, including a package of rugs he

[1] He was no relation to General William ("Wild Bill") Donovan, wartime head of the O.S.S.

had woven in a Soviet prison 1,200 miles from the Glienicker Bridge.

He was a mountain boy from Virginia who had flown
a strange black airplane twelve miles above the earth and
had come crashing down in the Urals, another chain of
mountains halfway around the world. He had been a prisoner among strangers for one year, nine months and nine
days.

His name was Francis Gary Powers.

It was after 2:00 A.M. in Washington, and the party
at the White House was in full swing. It was a private
gathering honoring the President's brother-in-law, Stephen
E. Smith, who was leaving his State Department post.
President Kennedy was tanned, relaxed, and cordial. He
drank ice water and did not dance, but he mingled continuously with his guests, chatting and smiling.

In the Blue Room, band leader Lester Lanin, a short,
bald man in tails, had kept the fox-trot music flowing
through the early part of the evening. Now the guests
were in a mood for some dignified twisting. Mrs. Jacque-
line Kennedy, lovely in a white sheath, danced occasionally and laughed when Oleg Cassini, her friend and dress
designer, did a twist at her request, a sort of Peppermint
Lounge kazatska.

The bar was set up in the doorway between the Red
Room and the Blue Room, serving champagne and whis-
key.

Despite the gay party atmosphere, some of the Cabinet members on the edges of the room seemed preoccupied. They stood in small knots in a semicircle, half-
watching the beautiful women on the dance floor, but

speaking tensely among themselves in whispers, about something else.

Vice-President Lyndon Johnson wore a blue dinner jacket, although everyone else was in black. Secretary of Defense Robert S. McNamara; Assistant to the President McGeorge Bundy—the guest list read like a meeting of the National Security Council. Their eyes were on the twisters, but their minds were on the Glienicker Bridge.

The society guests danced on, oblivious of what was happening; but to a handful of reporters invited to the party, Presidential news secretary Pierre Salinger quietly passed the word that something interesting might be announced about 2:30 A.M. He advised them not to leave. His office began routing other newsmen out of bed all over the capital.

At the center of the bridge, Donovan and Shishkin gingerly went through the first formalities of the exchange. Both Powers and Abel were identified, Powers by the C.I.A. agent and Abel by one of the Russians. Then came a delay until the Americans could verify that a third man, Frederic L. Pryor, had been released as agreed twelve miles away at the Friedrichstrasse crossing point between East and West Berlin. Pryor, a twenty-eight-year-old Yale graduate arrested the previous August by the East Germans, was a part of the three-way exchange. For twenty minutes the two groups waited at the white line. Finally, at 8:50 A.M., one of the Americans walked back out on the bridge with the message that Pryor had been set free.

In the Blue Room, Lester Lanin brought his hand down and the band broke into a lively melody. Scarcely anyone noticed that the President had slipped away to await a telephone call.

At the center of the Glienicker Bridge, the handcuffs were removed from Abel. He began moving forward. So did Powers. The two men passed each other as they stepped over the white line.

It was 8:52 A.M. in Berlin.

"Gee, I'm glad to see you," Powers said.

The C.I.A. was glad to see Francis Gary Powers. They had been waiting to question him for a long time . . .

►2

Flight

HE WAS THIRTY YEARS OLD AND he had flown more than five hundred hours in the U-2. He had completed twenty-seven missions in it since reporting to the Middle East four years before. Each had been a grueling and lonely ride along the edges of space. But the worst ride for any U-2 pilot was the silent flight over the Soviet Union.

Francis Gary Powers was flying there that day for the Central Intelligence Agency.

On his hip was a noiseless 22-caliber semiautomatic pistol.

In his logbook were the notations: 1 May 1960. Sortie Number 4154. Takeoff 0126 GMT [6:26 A.M. local time], delayed one-half hour.

On his map, a red and blue line traced a 3,788-mile

flight from Peshawar, Pakistan, to Bodo, Norway. It would take him 2,919 miles over the Soviet Union, past Stalinabad, Aralsk, Chelyabinsk, Sverdlovsk, Kirov, Archangel, and Murmansk.

He would fly at upwards of 70,000 feet through the hostile upper atmosphere where day begins to look like night and the outside temperature can drop to a hundred below zero.

Underneath him was the most sophisticated paraphernalia of modern electronic espionage—cameras, tape recorders, radios, radars. But the last thing that had been handed to him was as ancient and primitive as spying itself—a square piece of black cloth, a password for a jet-age sentry at the other end of a continent.

Powers edged the plane slowly along the runway. Its huge droopy wings extended eighty feet across, almost twice the length of its body. A man was perched halfway down each of them. As the plane picked up speed, they leaped to the ground and pulled the connecting pins from the removable wheels under the wings.

They waved the pins at Powers and he took his signal to turn on full power. Halfway down the runway the wheels fell away under the tug of gravity. Within seconds, the great glider jet was airborne and out of sight.

Powers identified himself on his radio—Puppy 68—and let the tower know he had managed the takeoff without mishap and was heading for target. He was not supposed to use the radio again for more than eight hours.

Below, fleetingly, were the Kabul River and the Khyber Pass, Russia's historic invasion route to the South. Powers pushed his speed past 400 mph and still in the takeoff climb crossed the Afghanistan border fifty miles to the north.

To the east, in the full light of morning, was China. To the west, through the dawning rays over the Middle East, was Europe in the dark of night. A hundred miles ahead was the Soviet Union, awake in Asia, asleep in Europe.

It was overcast, and the clouds covered the mighty Himalayas stretching eastward from the Hindukush range. In the distance, the highest mountains in the world soared 30,000 feet to the awesome peak at Karakorum.

Powers was already above it, still climbing, reaching for 60,000 feet to cross the Soviet border beyond the practical grasp of any of the world's fighter aircraft. The U-2 carried a granger to create artificial static for enemy radar and, as he approached the border, 190 miles north of the Afghan capital at Kabul, Powers switched it on.

The plane was headed straight for Tyura Tam, the Soviet Cape Canaveral, eighty miles to the east of the Aral Sea. Tyura Tam and Kapustin Yar, another test center southeast of Stalingrad, were the only intercontinental ballistic missile sites that American intelligence had located in the Soviet Union.

But on April 9, a U-2 had spotted traces of disturbing diggings along the route Powers was to follow that day. Local agents and electronic eavesdropping deepened suspicions that the Soviets were building their first operational ICBM base.

The primary purpose of the May 1 flight was to photograph the construction before the Russians could camouflage the site under cover of the thick fog which blankets the north of the Soviet Union in the summer months.

Powers checked his equipment. He was carrying a remarkable camera with a rotating 944.7-millimeter lens which peered out through seven holes in the belly of the plane. It would take 4,000 paired pictures of a 125-mile-wide, 2,174-mile-long strip of the Soviet Union.

The plane was also fitted with three tape recorders fed by antennae sprouting beneath the plane. They would sketch an electronic memo to the Strategic Air Command on the sound and location of Russian radio and radar stations.

It was 7:36 A.M. and Powers prepared to take a navigational fix by beaming his radio compass at a station near Stalinabad, ninety miles to the north. Below him was the border of the Soviet Union.

At Incirlik Air Base, ten miles from Adana, near the southern coast of Turkey, it was 4:36 A.M. Powers' twenty-four-year-old wife Barbara was asleep in trailer T1356 at the end of two even rows of twenty-two identical trailers flanking an asphalt road.

There, amid carefully clipped lawns, domesticated flowers and crawling vines, an isolated bit of middle-class suburbia had been created for the seven U-2 pilots, the supporting crews, and their wives and children. The terrain was as flat as the Great Plains back home, and the rugged Taurus Mountains thirty miles to the north provided the only break in a monotonous horizon.

This was the home of the top-secret 10-10 detachment which turned its face to the world as the Second Weather Observational Squadron (Provisional). Because of the enforced secrecy, its members broke all the rules of military base etiquette. The men shunned the officers' and noncommissioned officers' clubs, and the women shopped by themselves at the Commissary.

They were housed together, they spent their leisure together, their children played together on the asphalt street (of all the families only the Powerses were child-less). The wives comforted each other when the men were away on a mission, and they rejoiced when one of them could withdraw for a rare vacation.

Barbara, a lush Georgia girl, had only recently re-turned with Gary (as she called him) from the beach a hundred miles away and she was still hobbling on a walk-ing cast that covered the leg she had broken water skiing.

She had last seen her husband shortly after 6:00 P.M., Wednesday, April 27, when he left for the 2,100-mile flight by transport to Peshawar.

"Fix me a fair-size lunch," he had said, and, unques-tioningly, while he was packing his gear, she had prepared a Thermos of hot potato soup, a Thermos of coffee, six sandwiches—tuna fish, pimento cheese, Spam—some sweet pickles, olives and cookies.

In Istanbul, 425 miles to the northwest across the Turkish peninsula, Secretary of State Christian A. Herter was also asleep. He had arrived the night before, slipping through back streets to avoid the rioting against the top-pling regime of Adnan Menderes. He was there for a meeting of the Foreign Ministers of the North Atlantic Treaty Organization. He did not know another U-2 was in the air over the Soviet Union.

In Washington it was 10:36 P.M. Saturday night. At a supersecret operations center away from the main com-plex of C.I.A. buildings, the progress of Powers' flight was being recorded with pins on a map. The center had been notified as soon as the U-2 left Peshawar.

At Camp David, the Presidential retreat in Mary-land's Catoctin Mountains, President Eisenhower was re-laxing after a day of golf; he was unaware that Powers

was in the air. Eisenhower had concerned himself with
the broad outlines of the U-2 program, but left the details
to subordinates.

It was at Camp David on a weekend the previous
September that the President had met on intimate and
friendly terms with Nikita S. Khrushchev, the Soviet Premier. It seemed to be the beginning of a bright new
honeymoon in Russian-American relations.

Eisenhower was to carry the "Spirit of Camp David"
to Paris for a summit meeting two weeks hence. Then, as
Khrushchev's honored guest, he was to visit the Soviet
Union the following month.

In Pound, Virginia, in a hollow at the tapering tail of
the Appalachian Mountains, it was 9:36 P.M. The Powers
clan had withdrawn for the night into a cluster of primitive houses along a solitary dirt road.

They were of hill-country stock. Their forebears had
moved from Massachusetts in the eighteenth century,
escaping from British regulation into the fierce individualism of the frontier. Isolated by their mountains, cut off
from through roads, electricity, and the telephone until
thirty years ago, they turned in upon themselves. They
lived by the Bible and their own stern rules. Outsiders
were suspect. The world beyond was impious.

Francis Gary Powers was born to the life of the hills
shortly after 8:00 P.M., August 17, 1929, the second child
of Oliver and Ida Ford Powers. His birthplace was a
weary miner's house hard by the rail line in Camden, just
across the Kentucky border. His parents were convinced
the house was haunted and his mother carried him under
the pressure of that fear.

Oliver immediately set about ridding himself of the

place and managed the next year to swap it for a house in nearby Jenkins, Kentucky. It was the start of a migrancy which began in the depression and lasted through the war. It brought Francis (as his family called him) to six homes in four states in his first fifteen years.

Oliver went from the mines to the Army (he served as Pfc. for three years in Columbus, Georgia), back to the mines, into a small shoe repair business, up to Detroit for fat wartime wages as an electrical helper at the Great Lakes Steel Company, and back again to the hills and his shoemaking.

Oliver had never got past the fifth grade, but he had abundant native wit and his imagination stretched beyond his limited schooling and the narrow boundaries of the hills. Francis was his only son. Ida could raise their five girls, but the boy was his and he would fulfill his ambition in him.

Francis was a quiet boy and a good boy. He lived faithfully under the Biblical injunction of filial piety. He helped his father and his grandfather farm their small patch of land. He went regularly each Sunday to the fundamentalist Church of Christ, which his family attended, or to the Baptist Church.

He loved to hunt and fish, mainly by himself. A good athlete, particularly at individual sports such as track, he grew up lean and hard and good-looking.

He did moderately well in his studies without much effort. He finished twenty-second in a class of sixty-nine at Grundy High School (he had a 96 in physics). On the side, he read a good deal more than the other boys. When something was troubling him, he'd go to his room, stretch out on his bed and read a book. He liked Zane Grey and for background music he was likely to choose a Strauss waltz for the record player.

None of his schoolmates was really close to him. They remember him only as an unobtrusive, well-mannered boy who kept to himself. He was never heard to utter a word of profanity. He didn't smoke. He didn't drink. He didn't chew.

Until he left for Milligan College, just across the Tennessee border in Johnson City, he never had a formal date. But he'd sometimes go on a group picnic with a local girl, and he was twice on the verge of marriage before he met Barbara.

Francis had a normal boyhood fondness for movies about pilots and their adventures in the air. He tinkered with model airplanes like millions of others. And for Valentine's Day he gave his fifth-grade teacher a plane he had fashioned from a cigar box.

But his lasting fascination with flying began when he was fourteen and passing through Princeton, West Virginia, on a family outing. Francis persuaded Oliver to let him go up in a two-seater with a woman pilot. She liked the boy and cut the five-dollar fee in half. He liked the experience.

"I left my heart up there, Pap," Oliver recalled him saying, "and I'm goin' back to git it."

Francis had become restless in the hills and he would pace the floor of his father's house, jingling coins in his pocket.

"It's a shame," he would say. "There's nothing left in the world to explore."

"He done what he was told," Oliver remembered. "But he was an adventuresome boy. He never wanted to fly with more than one person in the plane. He was a nervous boy, too."

Alone in his plane over the Soviet Socialist Republic of Tadzikstan, Powers was nervously throwing the mission switches at the designated points on his map.

He was five feet nine and a half and weighed 165 pounds—the ideal size for the cramped cockpit of the U-2. But even for him, it was a cruel plane. He would say that he "believed in it," much as a man might state an article of faith. But a pilot could have no true affection for it.

For more than eight hours he would be gripped by the ugly pressure suit, living on pure oxygen in a discomforting caricature of breathing, forced to great exertion to accomplish the simplest motions.

Below, the earth was covered by thick clouds, as if all life had been blotted out. Yet he knew the Soviet Air Defense Command would be alive with activity. The United States had been flying into Soviet air space with impunity since the end of World War II. Stripped-down B-36 bombers started making short penetrations just after the war, and by 1950 the RB-47, a reconnaissance version of the bomber, was conducting scheduled intrusions. In one twenty-four-hour period seventeen of them had been over the Soviet Union.

Overflights had been tried with camera-laden balloons, lofted on the prevailing easterly winds from U.S. bases in Germany. But it was not until the Lockheed Aircraft Corporation had the first U-2 flying in August of 1955 that an effective and controlled program of overflight became a possibility.

From the outset the U-2 overflights were run with the full knowledge of the British government and the full co-operation of British intelligence. The first "cover" operation overseas was conducted out of a U.S. Air Force base at Lakenheath, Suffolk, to which the U-2 was assigned early in 1956 as part of purported "Meteorological research." And British agents inside the Soviet Union often provided intelligence tips which led to U-2 over-flights.

The Russians made sporadic protests, but more often they maintained an indignant silence because they could do nothing about it. The U-2 brought back photographs of Soviet fighters rising to the attack only to mush out hopelessly before they reached the exalted altitude of the "black lady of espionage"—as it was called in their military journals.

But operating under a top priority provoked by the U-2 flights, the Soviet Air Defense Command had been making significant advances in radar detection and anti-aircraft missilery. Now, berated by Khrushchev for having failed to bring down the previous U-2 flight, they had locked on Powers' plane the moment it crossed the border.

And, in turn, the United States was tracking him on its network of powerful radar stations along the perimeter of the Iron Curtain.

Powers was preoccupied by the precise skills of his trade—keeping an exact course, throwing the mission switches near important targets, marking unusual weather on the map, hoarding the precious fuel supply by gliding long stretches, engine idling.

He was a first-rate pilot, a superb navigator, and an exceptional photographer. He had always followed his instructions to the letter and he was doing so that day. But he was under an inexplicable anxiety that he had not felt on his previous flights.

After arriving in Peshawar with about twenty members of the supporting crew, Powers and another U-2 pilot had been subjected to a routine preflight psychological examination. The prime ingredient of a successful overflight was a pilot's confidence in himself, his plane, and his equipment. The test was to determine who would make the overflight and who would fly a decoy mission along the Soviet border and back to Turkey. The two men had been awakened three and a half hours before takeoff, served breakfast, and given their assignments. Powers was told he was to make the overflight.

Later, Allen W. Dulles,[1] Director of the C.I.A., studied the results of the psychological tests and decided that, had he been the agent on the scene, he would not have sent Powers over the Soviet Union that day.

Dulles realized that some U-2 pilots were worried about the workings of the destruction system in the plane. In the event of trouble over the Soviet Union—they were told—it would destroy the evidence after the pilot had tossed himself clear in his ejection seat.

But if the plane were hit by enemy fire or developed engine trouble of its own, could a pilot be sure the delicate timing mechanism would work? Could he be sure an injured plane would give him the precious seconds he needed to eject himself safely? Could he be sure there would be any time lag at all?

In front of Powers was a switch marked "Explosion." Behind him, just to the rear of the cockpit, was a model 175-10A destructor unit with a three-pound charge of

---

[1] Dulles retired November 29, 1961, and was succeeded by John A. McCone.

cyclonite. It was powerful enough to destroy the plane and everything in it.[2]

If he was trapped in the sky or on the soil of the Soviet Union, Powers' instructions were to make sure the plane was destroyed. He could do it by activating the timer, throwing the explosion switch and ejecting. Or if the evidence could be removed with certainty in no other way, he could throw the explosion switch alone and destroy both the plane and himself.

No one had ever told him to commit suicide (scruples aside, the C.I.A. didn't think the "Kamikaze principle" would work with American pilots). But he had been impressed with the necessity of destroying the evidence.

Powers had not been subjected to the long and exacting psychological, ideological and professional training of a C.I.A. agent. Men who were willing and able to fly the U-2 were scarce in 1955 and they were needed right away.

In the recruitment of the U-2 pilots the primary requirement was that they be good aviators. But selections were made with great care, nonetheless. All of the highly developed techniques of the government's security agencies were employed to eliminate risks.

The C.I.A. recognized that in an age of "truth serums" and sophisticated torture a prisoner could be made to talk. But Powers, like all U-2 pilots, was instructed to try to limit his disclosures to what the Russians might surmise on their own. He was told to say as little as possible each time he was interrogated. But he could tell what he knew,

---

[2] In the report it issued after Powers was released, the C.I.A. said "the purpose of the destruct mechanism was to render inoperable the precision camera and other equipment, not to destroy them and the film."

Army Ordnance, on the other hand, describes cyclonite, also known as RDX, as one of the most powerful explosives in the world. Three pounds of it could blow up four trucks.

bit by bit, to ward off drugs or torture. The idea was to buy time in the hope that the grilling would stop before the Russians learned everything.[3]

He was given Escape and Evasion Training, however, to reduce the chances of capture. And in his pocket, along with 7,500 Soviet rubles and other currency, was a silver dollar piece with an inch-and-a-quarter pin hidden inside. The pin in turn held a needle tipped with a fatal dose of curare, a deadly poison. It could kill a dog in three minutes, a mouse in twenty seconds.

He had been given the pin, Powers was told, to enable him to take his own life were he to crash in an isolated area, injured and in agony, or were he to be subjected to torture upon capture.

In the matter-of-fact parlance of the intelligence men, suicide was optional. But could a man take his own life? And did he have a right to?

"If you kill yourself, you kill a man," Oliver told the boy when he was turning eighteen. "A man who dies in sin, he can't be saved. Christ said, 'Upon this rock I will build my Church.' He's the ruler of the Church on earth. It's a sin to kill yourself. The last act you do, if it's sinful, you go into discard."

Oliver was a religious man, and when the time came for the boy to go away, he was happy to see him enter Milligan College. It was a church school and Bible study was a required course for at least one year.

[3] The version of the instructions given in the C.I.A. report was that the U-2 pilots were to "adopt a cooperative attitude toward their captors [and feel] perfectly free to tell the full truth about their mission with the exception of certain specifications of the aircraft."

During his appearance before the Senate Armed Services Committee on March 6, 1962, Powers was asked to state his instructions. When he said it was "hard to remember," the committee directed him to read the version in the C.I.A. report into the record.

Francis had shown no great interest in going to college, but Oliver was insistent. From his Army days he remembered that with a good education a man could become an officer.

"I wanted him to go to college," Oliver recalled, "because I was afraid that was all I could give him."

Oliver paid all of Francis' bills except for the $600 the boy provided in his junior year out of the $1,300 he made the previous summer working at the Bristol Steel Company's Mead Forks tipple.

Francis' academic record at Milligan was as ordinary as the one he left behind at Grundy High. Of the fifty-nine students in the graduating class of 1950, he again ranked twenty-second. But his grades as a pre-medical student were good enough to have gained him admission to any of the nearby medical schools.

"They never did catch him studying," Oliver was to say with a touch of admiration. "I wanted him to be a doctor, but he said he'd rather be a·pilot."

As he had in his early years, Francis kept to himself at college. When enticed into a campus bull session, he was genial and expressive. But he rarely started a conversation and he is remembered by his classmates principally as a quiet young man perpetually wearing a white T-shirt.

Rigorous about diet and physical fitness, he shunned medicine, even aspirin. He kept in splendid physical condition, mainly as the result of solitary, hour-long exercises in his room. His companions in Pardee Hall needled him about it. But they did it good-naturedly, for they were fond of him in a distant sort of way and they respected him. None has ever spoken a word against him.

Francis ran the 100 and the 220 for the track team and competed one year in the Penn relays. He was a better than average college athlete with a peculiar, purposeful style. Most men run with their hands relaxed or clenched in a fist. Francis extended his fingers stiffly and cut into the wind sharply with his hand as if he were solving an aerodynamic problem.

Most of the things he did well, he did on his own. Once while "spelunking" in the local mountains, Francis and a few of his professors found themselves lost in a complicated cave. While the others debated what to do, he retraced his steps to a spot where he remembered dropping a candy wrapper. Then he returned to the party and led them out.

* * *

As he approached the Aral Sea, the weather cleared for a short stretch and Powers could see he had drifted to the right of course. He was correcting back when he spotted the condensation trails of a jet paralleling his course at a considerably lower altitude. Although he did not think it had seen him, it was his first sign that the Russians might have had him spotted.

He had been in the air for more than two hours, and it was then that the pressure suit started to take its toll. He had been suffering of late from severe head and ear aches, provoked by the artificial intake of oxygen during his eight- to nine-hour flights.

His neck had been rubbed raw by the cork ring which served as the hermetic seal for his helmet. (Often it would draw blood. The slightest wrinkle in the pressure suit would pinch at him hour upon hour, raising blood blisters and welts. He was wearing his long-legged underwear inside out to keep the seams away from his body, but the best of precautions could not prevent him from being cut and bruised by every abrupt movement in the suit.)

The oxygen system forced him to reverse the normal process of breathing. Instead of exerting himself to inhale, he had to use pressure to exhale. He had not drawn a natural breath for close to five hours now. He had been called to the Pre-Breathing Room just after breakfast and he had been inside the helmet since 4:30 A.M.

He was pumped full of oxygen as his commanding officer, Colonel William M. Shelton,[4] went over the map and gave him his final instructions.

The weather, which was the controlling factor in decisions at Shelton's level, had taken a slight turn for the better. It had been perfect all the way across the Soviet Union on April 28, but Powers had not yet completed his preflight examination. On the twenty-ninth it snowed near Sverdlovsk and on the thirtieth it was cloudy along most of the route. The flight had to be canceled.

The weather prediction for May 1 left something to be desired, but there was no assurance it would get any better. Shelton decided to send the flight then.

He was able to conduct the briefing in just an hour and a quarter, for Powers was an old hand and well acquainted with the difficult landing procedure at Bodo. He had flown a U-2 there from Adana in August of 1958 by way of Greece, Italy, and West Germany. Then he had spent two or three weeks studying the landing conditions at the Bodo airfield in preparation for future flights.

When Shelton's briefing was completed, two personal-equipment specialists helped Powers hoist on his pressure suit. Then he held his breath while they switched him

---

[4] A fellow Virginian from Keeling, Shelton was a much-decorated combat pilot in World War II and flew 100 missions in Korea. He was subsequently transferred to the 507th Fighter Wing at Kincheloe Air Force Base, Michigan.

C

from the main oxygen system to the walk-around bottle. At the rarefied altitudes of his flight plan, the slightest portion of nitrogen from the air could rack his body with the bends.

He lumbered from the Pre-Breathing Room to the "meat wagon," a truck which rushed him to his waiting plane at the end of the runway. Within minutes he had been strapped into the cockpit—he was too restricted by his suit to do it himself—and the plane was airborne.

Now, on the approach to the Ural Mountains, Powers had been without food for five hours and he would not have food or drink until he landed in another six or seven. He was a thousand miles from Peshawar and, at 1,700 miles, he was equidistant from the far border of the Soviet Union and his trailer at Adana.

Barbara had been spending the four long days since Gary's departure lolling in the sun and playing bridge with the other wives. There was an unspoken rule among them that they would avoid gossip about their husbands' missions.

"If the next-door neighbor asks you what your middle name is," they would remind each other half in jest, "it's time to move out."

Barbara had learned not to ask questions, but she had never been in doubt as to the nature of Gary's work. Before he entered the U-2 program he had asked her consent, and when he was sent overseas she was aware that he would become involved in the overflight program.

She had been a dutiful pilot's wife through nearly five years of marriage. She had been introduced to Gary by her mother, Monteen Brown, who met him while working in the cafeteria at Turner Air Force base in Albany,

Georgia, near their home in Milledgeville.

Powers was stationed there as a first lieutenant, flying the F-84 jet with the 468th Strategic Fighter Squadron of the 508th Bomber Wing.

He had entered the Air Force as an enlisted man in October of 1950 after a summer as a lifeguard at the Kiwanis Club pool in Jenkins—waiting out the draft.

He was trained as a photographer and served briefly at Westover Field, Massachusetts, before taking his flight training at Greenville Air Force Base, Mississippi. He got his wings and his commission in December of 1952 and took advanced and jet training at Williams Air Force Base, Chandler, Arizona, and Luke Air Force Base, Phoenix. Then, after a brief tour of noncombat duty in Japan during the Korean War, Powers reported to Turner late in 1953.

He had been there for less than three years when the C.I.A. spotted his qualifications and offered him a job— in addition to his photographic training, he had proved himself an excellent pilot and he was one of the six best gunners in the wing.

Powers quit his $700-a-month job with the Air Force in April of 1956 and went to work for Lockheed, which was serving as a front for the C.I.A., at a salary of $2,500 a month.[5] He reported as Francis Gary "Palmer" for training with the First Weather Observational Squadron (Provisional) at Watertown Strip, Nevada. And the following August 17—on his twenty-seventh birthday—he said goodby to his parents in Pound and left for Adana.

Barbara was not allowed to join him, but she secured

[5] Each month $1,000 was withheld, pending the fulfillment of the secret contract. Powers signed a second two-year contract in May of 1958 and renewed it for another year in January of 1960.

a job as an Air Force secretary in Greece and he managed
to fly to see her once or twice a month. In 1958 she received permission to live in Adana and the next year they
moved into the 10-10 compound at Incirlik. It was the
closest thing to a home they had known together.

Gary had been baptized as a Methodist in Barbara's
church in Milledgeville, Georgia, and now they attended the nondenominational Protestant services at the Air
Base on Sunday. There one weekend Gary met Burton B.
Thurston, a minister of the Christian Church and a friend
of Dr. Dean Walker, president of Milligan. He was teach-
ing at the American University in Lebanon and had been
asked to conduct the services at Adana that Sunday.

Except for such rare intrusions from a more familiar
world, life at Incirlik was confining and monotonous.
Even the PX failed to provide the accustomed comforts
of prepackaged America. Barbara complained that it was
good for little beyond bare necessities. There wasn't even
any Crisco or mayonnaise.

Still, the young couple had more money than they
had ever thought it was possible to earn. And in those
rare periods when he had leave, they could travel in expansive style. They came to know the pleasures of Europe,
and the excitement of slipping out of Beirut when the
U.S. Marines landed in 1958.

The overflight of May 1 was part of the price Barbara
and Gary had to pay for that good life.

Near Aralsk, Powers had turned the plane a few degrees to the north, and now he was well up the Siberian
side of the Urals. There were scattered low cumulus clouds
but the weather was clear and cloudless ahead.

Part of the route was marked on his map in blue

pencil, indicating the points where he might deviate without missing crucial targets. Where it was marked in red, he was to maintain the course without fail. It was so marked near Sverdlovsk.

There, surrounded by dense forests of birch and pine, a mighty industrial city had been built on the low-lying hills sloping from the mountains into the West Siberian plain. It was founded as Ekaterinberg in 1722 by Peter the Great. Czar Nicholas II and his family were murdered there by the Bolsheviks in 1918.

Sverdlovsk became a great city in World War II, when it was transformed into a mighty supplier for the Russian military machine. Now it was a principal center for the production of copper, chemicals, electronics, plastics, and rubber. And it was the largest rail and air transportation hub in the Urals.

An inevitable target in the event of war, it was encircled by the latest Soviet antiaircraft rockets. They were deployed in domed, igloo-like launch points, markedly different from the herringbone pattern of other, less advanced ground-to-air missile sites in the Soviet Union. Vice-President Richard M. Nixon had taken note of them during his visit to the city the previous July.

It was 10:30 A.M. as Powers neared Chelyabinsk, 125 miles to the south of the city. The unusual anxiety was still upon him and now the automatic pilot was beginning to act up. He decided to take a bearing with his radio compass.

He would need an exact navigational fix to follow the red line across the rocket batteries and over Sverdlovsk.

3

May Day

ON A QUIET, TREE-LINED
street in Georgetown, Washington's most fashionable resi-
dential section, a telephone rang at 11:15 A.M., the first
of May, in the home of Hugh S. Cumming, Jr.,[1] chief of
Intelligence and Research of the United States Department of State. A maid answered.

Because it was Sunday, Cumming, a distinguished,
white-haired member of one of Virginia's oldest families,
was in church. He was, as usual, at St. Paul's Episcopal,
several blocks from his home.

---

[1] Cumming was the son of an honest man in the Harding Administration,
Surgeon General Hugh S. Cumming. His father achieved fame when he
cracked down on the theft of bedsheets and supplies from a Veterans Hospital at Perryville, Maryland, ending a sort of medical Teapot Dome.

Not until he returned to his house on O Street shortly after noon did Cumming learn that a man had called and was urgently trying to reach him. From the name, Cumming knew what it might be; the caller was his C.I.A. contact for the U-2 operation.

The Cummings' coal-black dachshund, Gretchen, watched as her master dialed.

"Our boy isn't there," the voice on the other end of the line said carefully. "We don't know what happened to him." Although the conversation would have been meaningless to anyone listening, its import was chillingly clear to Cumming:

The U-2 was overdue at Bodo; it was presumed down, probably somewhere in the Soviet Union. The fate of the plane and pilot was unknown. Cumming had been the first official of the State Department notified by the C.I.A.

Allen Dulles did not yet know. He was, on Sunday morning, in the Grand Ballroom of the Waldorf-Astoria in New York City, receiving the Golden Rule Award "for distinguished government service and dedication to Christian ideals" from the New York Police Department's St. George Society.

For the moment, at least, Cumming was the official who had to act. A career diplomat who served two years in Moscow, he had been intelligence chief of the State Department since October, 1957. He was, in effect, the department's Dulles.

Outwardly he had the mild appearance and manner of an English country vicar. But the appearance was deceptive. When a United States C-130 transport crashed in Soviet Armenia September 2, 1958, Cumming had dropped out of sight in Washington for a few days.

He turned up in Turkey, flew over the Trebizond

beacon and along the Soviet border, retracing the C-130's route in an effort to find out what had happened.

Before doing so Cumming arranged to have it deliberately leaked to the Russians that he was aboard the plane, to see whether they would dare to shoot it down. When he surfaced in Washington without mishap, his Georgetown neighbors probably assumed he had spent the weekend pruning rosebushes in Virginia.

Although his name was unknown to the general public, Cumming was one of a handful of men at the State Department who knew the secret of the U-2.

Now, in his Georgetown home, Cumming picked up the telephone again and prepared to call Loy Henderson, who he assumed was Acting Secretary of State that day.

But an unnerving thought struck as he reached out to dial, and he placed the receiver back on its cradle.

The head of the State Department's intelligence service was faced with a curious dilemma. So secret was the U-2 program that Henderson, although a high official, was not among those authorized to know anything about it.

Cumming knew he must report the failure of the U-2 flight—but whom could he tell?

The U-2 overflights were, in the language of the intelligence world, so "black" that communication among the small group of men who ran the program was mostly by word of mouth. At the State Department, among those few officials who knew were Secretary Herter and Douglas Dillon, the urbane Under Secretary whom Herter had edged out for the top post a year earlier, shortly before the death of John Foster Dulles.

But Herter was in Istanbul. And Dillon, who had been in New Orleans Saturday morning, was still away, or so Cumming believed. He decided to check further, how-

ever, and was relieved to discover that Dillon had in fact
returned. He immediately telephoned him at his home on
Belmont Road. Both men realized they were talking over
a non-secure, ordinary phone line. Although they spoke
in guarded fashion, they reached an important decision,
the first of many that were to be reached in the days
ahead.

Since mid-1956, when U-2's began overflying the
Soviet Union, the C.I.A. had ready prepackaged "cover"
stories to suit the circumstances and the geography. These
were innocuous, short announcements to be plucked out
of the files and issued by Air Force public information
officers at local bases if and when a U-2 failed to come
back from a secret mission.

Both Dillon and Cumming knew that the prepared
cover story for the May 1 flight said that a weather plane
had taken off from Turkey and—without authorization—
wandered over Pakistan. For diplomatic reasons, the two
men now agreed that any mention of Pakistan, the real
jumping-off point for the flight, would have to be dropped
out of the cover story that would soon be issued to the
world.

Cumming was instructed to argue this view at a top-
secret C.I.A. meeting being held that afternoon to decide
the next move in a dangerous game.

Dulles, after delivering the speech to the policemen
in New York, flew back to the capital. He did not learn
that the U-2 was missing until he arrived at his home at
2723 Q Street, in Georgetown, between 2:00 and 3:00 P.M.

By this time the C.I.A. had notified Cumming, the
Pentagon, and the White House. Brigadier General Andrew J. Goodpaster, White House staff secretary, passed
the word along to Eisenhower at Camp David.

All this, of course, was going on behind the scenes. The public knew nothing yet.

And not even the highest officials in Washington, including Dulles, Dillon, and Cumming, had any way of learning the fate of the dark plane with the outsized wings or of its thirty-year-old pilot.

In Moscow, at 8:50 A.M. local time, the area around Red Square was jammed with humanity. At that moment Francis Gary Powers was nearing Sverdlovsk, 800 miles to the east of the Russian capital.

May Day in Moscow is a grimly festive occasion. The Soviet Union parades its armed might past carefully watching Western military attachés. Traditionally the leaders of the Soviet Union review the parade perched atop what was, on May Day of 1960, still designated the Lenin-Stalin tomb.

The parade started, as always, precisely at 10:00 A.M. The military units began moving smartly past the rotund figure of Soviet Premier Nikita S. Khrushchev, who stood on the red granite tomb with the bulldog-faced Soviet Defense Minister, Rodion Y. Malinovsky, the elderly Kliment Y. Voroshilov, President of the Presidium of the Supreme Soviet, and Otto Grotewohl, Premier of Communist East Germany. Incongruously, a group of little children occupied places of honor just in front of them.

Among the Western diplomats watching the parade was Llewellyn E. Thompson, a skilled envoy with a wrinkled, grandfatherly face and clear blue eyes. Thompson was on friendly personal terms with Khrushchev; he had worked long to improve relations between Washington and Moscow.

On this May Day, too, the world was poised on the

eve of a great summit conference between the leaders of the United States, the Soviet Union, Britain, and France.

Thompson was hopeful that the goal toward which he had worked—some easing of the tensions that could lead to world destruction—was within reach.

Forty-five minutes after the start of the parade, Thompson noticed a commotion on the reviewing stand atop the tomb. Marshal Konstantin A. Vershinin, commander-in-chief of the Soviet Air Force, arrived late, entered at the rear of the stand, and whispered to Khrushchev. There was a brief, intense huddle of top Soviet officials while the parade continued. Thompson was curious, but had no way of knowing what it was all about.

Later, looking back, Thompson was convinced that he had witnessed the moment when Khrushchev learned that the U-2 would never finish its mission and was, in fact, down on Soviet territory near Sverdlovsk.

At Camp David, it was raining this morning of May 1. Eisenhower had golfed in nearby Gettysburg the day before with his son, Major John S. D. Eisenhower, his twelve-year-old grandson, David, and George Allen, perennial friend of Presidents. Because it rained on Sunday, he canceled plans for early church and a round of golf afterwards.

He decided to go back to the White House in the afternoon.

The rain in Washington had stopped in mid-morning, but it was cloudy in the capital, and stayed that way well into the early afternoon. By this time other high officials of the government had been alerted by the C.I.A. The

intelligence agency had received the news from halfway
around the world over its own protected communications
network, after agents at Bodo, Incirlik and Peshawar
realized there was no longer even a slim hope that Powers
would come gliding in to the airfield at the tiny fishing
village on the Norwegian sea.

Besides Dulles, Cumming, and Dillon, the Secretary
of Defense, Thomas S. Gates, Jr., was notified that the U-2
was overdue. So was Dr. Hugh L. Dryden, Deputy Administrator of the National Aeronautics and Space Administration, a scholarly scientist with snowy hair, thick
bifocals, and a precise manner.

Dryden was a devout Methodist who had put himself
through college by preaching on the side, and still occasionally took the pulpit of his church in Washington. He
was telephoned because he was a key figure in the U-2
espionage program from the start.

Much later, fanciful tales were to circulate on the
Washington cocktail circuit that C.I.A. had brilliantly de-
ceived NASA into believing the U-2 flew only "weather"
missions. Nothing could be further from the truth. Dryden
had in fact willingly allowed NASA and its precursor
agency, the National Advisory Committee for Aeronautics,
to be used as the C.I.A.'s cover from the very start of the
project. He felt it his patriotic duty, and had no regrets
about it later.

He knew the full scope of the risky espionage program, as did three other key men at NASA. One of them
was soon to wish he didn't.

In Georgetown, the early afternoon sun was breaking
through the overcast as Cumming drove to the C.I.A.
meeting that would shape the precise language of the

cover story. He headed for the building in downtown Washington where Powers' flight progress had been plotted.

The exact location of this building is classified information, but it can be said that it is not far from the White House. To the shopkeepers and others in the area, the C.I.A. agents going in and out of the building are simply businessmen and secretaries.

The conference there took place in a setting that resembled the war briefing room familiar to all devotees of British spy films, even to a huge wall map and pointers.

Cumming was the only State Department man present. The rest were C.I.A. officials and technical experts. The men who gathered around the table this afternoon were concerned, but not overly so. True, there was every indication that Powers was down in the Soviet Union, but the chances that the Russians would recover any damning physical evidence of the overflight were slim. As the program had developed over four years, the C.I.A. had sought to improve the technical ability of U-2 pilots to destroy the evidence, and Powers, it was assumed, had successfully followed his orders to destroy the plane in case of trouble. If he were alive, a pilot without a plane can be disowned.

The discussion, therefore, centered on the cover story. One had to be issued, the C.I.A. felt, because a NASA "weather" plane had taken off and failed to return to base. It would seem suspicious to conceal this fact, since the program was ostensibly innocent. Also, a "search" must be started for the missing weather plane.

It was for just such emergencies, of course, that the C.I.A. had cover stories in its files. In intelligence parlance, a cover story is a euphemism for a lie, or partial lie. Like most lies, a cover story has a specific purpose—to protect the mission, the agent, the nation that has sent the spy out on the mission, and its intelligence apparatus.

The cover story pulled out of the files on May 1 and under consideration by the men meeting at the clandestine C.I.A. headquarters stated that the U-2 had taken off from Turkey on an upper-altitude-research mission and had, unfortunately, overflown Pakistan without authorization after the pilot reported mechanical difficulty.

Cumming vehemently argued against any mention of Pakistan. His words carried the authority of Dillon, the Acting Secretary. Cumming maintained that there were overriding political reasons to make no mention of Pakistan, partly because of its exposed geographical position, on the flank of both the Soviet Union and Communist China.

Dillon and Cumming, in their telephone conversation earlier in the afternoon, had discussed which country could best stand the furor if a storm arose over the flight. They reached the conclusion that the Turks, a traditionally tough and independent-minded people, could take the international political pressure better than the Pakistanis.

Cumming prevailed, and the C.I.A. agreed to drop Pakistan from the cover story. But this was only the beginning of their task. With Pakistan out, a new flight plan had to be agreed upon for the cover.

In working out a plausible, but thoroughly bogus, flight plan for the U-2, the men in the war-room setting were restricted by the fact that the U-2's height, range, and fuel capacity were top secret. The cover story, therefore, had somehow to fall within the limits of previously published data on the U-2, including the 1959 edition of Jane's *All the World's Aircraft.*

According to Jane's the U-2 was a weather-research craft capable of maintaining an altitude no higher than 55,000 feet.[2] Other published data said the plane could fly up to four hours. This, naturally, was a masterpiece of understatement, but it restricted the creative abilities of the men working on the cover story this Sunday afternoon.

With slide rules, calipers, and maps, the technical experts then worked out an altered version, eliminating Pakistan and setting forth a triangular flight plan skirting the Soviet border but entirely within Turkey.

Their work finished, the officials present gave their final approval to the revised cover story. It was dispatched by C.I.A. closed communications to various key points, including Adana, where it was to be given out to the press if questions were asked.

It was also transmitted to the Secretary of State.

At Camp David it was still midafternoon. Eisenhower had been scheduled to motor from his mountain retreat at 3:30 P.M. At the last moment he changed his mind and flew back to the White House by helicopter. Mrs. George Allen and Mrs. Eisenhower returned to Washington by car. The President's wife did not like to fly.

May 1 was in its waning hours at Khabarovsk, near the Manchurian border, when Count Guido Piovene, an Italian author and journalist, and his blond, modish wife, Mimi, climbed aboard a Tupelov jet with fifty-eight other passengers and headed west toward Irkutsk, en route to Moscow.

[2] Advanced models of the U-2, such as the one flown by Powers, actually had a ceiling of over 80,000 feet.

Piovene, once known as the "Conte Rosso," the Red Count, because of his postwar, and since modified, political leanings, was ending a trip through the Soviet Union with his wife and an interpreter assigned by Moscow.

They flew across the Soviet heartland to Irkutsk, and then to Omsk, where they remained an hour and a half while the pilots demanded, waited for, and were served a hot meal. The plane took off again, this time, the Piovenes were told, for Moscow.

Instead, the commercial Soviet airliner landed in the darkness at a strange airport. "We are in Sverdlovsk," the stewardess told the Piovenes. "Stay on the plane. Do not disembark." She spoke softly so as not to awaken the other passengers, most of whom were asleep.

At dawn, Mimi Piovene gazed out the window of the plane as the sun burst over the Urals, revealing that the mountains encircled the airport in a U-shape. Then she blinked in surprise, for very near the airliner was what she later termed "a beautiful white plane," with long wings and no markings. Curious, Mrs. Piovene, through her interpreter, asked one of the airliner's pilots about it.

"Oh yes," he replied casually, "it's a test plane."

Mrs. Piovene was intrigued because she had taken flying lessons as a girl and had more than a passing interest in airplanes. Soon the airliner took off, and this time made it to Moscow. But the odd appearance of the plane she had seen at Sverdlovsk stuck in Mimi Piovene's mind.

Istanbul on May 1 was a city under martial law.

Herter was weary from a long day of private conversations with the British and French, in advance of the next day's NATO meeting.

For three days now, there had been student riots

against the repressive Menderes regime, and its downfall
was only twenty-six days off. Tanks and troops armed with
tommy guns patrolled the streets, and Western diplomats
needed yellow stickers on their cars to move about after
curfew.

It was nightfall now in Istanbul, once Byzantium.
From the window of his eighth-floor suite in the Istanbul
Hilton, Herter could see the lights of half a dozen freight-
ers anchored in the Bosporus.

The C.I.A.'s coded message was on its way to the
ancient city on the Golden Horn, where Europe and Asia
almost touch. The vast, interlocking intelligence and diplomatic machinery of the United States government was
moving, but like a fogbound ship on a collision course.

Black as a Hat

THE U-2 WAS EXPECTED TO live as a spy plane for perhaps a year. It proved much more durable. But those who gave it life had no illusions about its end.

It was born in the last days of October, 1954, in Room 4E964, an office in the Pentagon, overlooking the Potomac. Its fathers had been fretting about it for three months and one of them finally became exasperated.

"Let's stop talking about it," he said, "and build the damn plane."

The scene was the office of Trevor Gardner, a thirty-nine-year-old engineering prodigy who had been persuaded by President Eisenhower to join the government in 1953 as a technical adviser to the Air Force on research and development. He made a dramatic exit three years later when the Administration refused to provide more money for bombers and missiles.

Gardner was a member of a small group which had been agonizing over the U-2 since July. The idea had been brought to the Air Force by Clarence L. (Kelly) Johnson, a Lockheed vice-president and its chief designer.

In December, 1953, Johnson had begun an investigation of the possibility of increasing the performance of his F-104 jet so as to gain maximum altitude and range for reconnaissance purposes. He decided quickly that an entirely new plane might be built to snoop at will on the Soviet Union.

On March 5, 1954, Johnson took his design to Gardner and Colonel Bernard A. Schriever, who was later to become the chief of all missile development in the Air Force. They liked the idea and advised Johnson to draw up a formal plan.

Early the next month, he submitted a full description of the plan along with a suggested program of construction. He was supported by Gardner and his deputy, Garrison Norton. But there was an uncertain reaction among the military men present, Lieutenant General Donald L. Putt, Deputy Chief of Staff for Development, and three of his assistants.

On June 7, 1954, Johnson's idea was rejected in a letter from Major General Floyd Wood, Deputy Commander for Technical Operations of the Air Research and Development Command.

The proposal was revived by the Science Advisory Committee, which had been established by the White House to explore new scientific techniques for the government. Gardner had submitted Johnson's plan and it was endorsed by Edwin H. Land, Edward M. Purcell, and John Tukey,[1] members of a subcommittee looking into intelligence and reconnaissance.

Johnson was called back to Washington on November 19, 1954, and questioned in great detail by Gardner and the three scientists. He also discussed the project over lunch with Harold Talbott, the Secretary of the Air Force, Allen Dulles,and Richard M.Bissell,[2] who had been brought into the C.I.A. that year as a troubleshooter and idea man.

As a boy Bissell used to memorize railroad timetables and he still retained a fascination for details. He was one of the new breed of intelligence operatives, a tall, lean man with subdued Ivy League clothes and thin horn-rimmed glasses. A forty-five-year-old Connecticut Yankee (his father was president of the Hartford Insurance Company), he was educated at Groton and Yale, took advanced study at the London School of Economics, and received his Ph.D. at Yale in 1939.

He became a professor of economics at Yale, then at the Massachusetts Institute of Technology. On various leaves of absence he served in Washington with the Commerce Department, the War Shipping Administration, and the Office of War Mobilization and Reconversion. In 1948 he joined the Marshall Plan and rose to the rank of acting administrator.

Bissell was intrigued by Johnson's proposal and joined

[1] Land headed the Polaroid Corporation, which he organized in 1937. He developed the Polaroid camera and many other photographic innovations. Purcell was a Nobel prize-winning physics professor at the Massachusetts Institute of Technology, Tukey a mathematics professor at Princeton.
[2] Bissell, who directed the C.I.A.'s unsuccessful invasion of Cuba in April, 1961, resigned early in 1962. In March of that year he became executive vice-president of the Institute for Defense Analyses, a private research organization conducting consulting work for the government. The head of I.D.A. was Garrison Norton, Gardner's former deputy.

forces with Gardner and the scientists in pushing it. A plane that could fly at 70,000 feet—Johnson's first goal—was a fantastic idea in 1954. The top operating altitude for aircraft at that time was 50,000 feet. The British had just set a record—54,000 feet on a zoom-up. But Johnson had done fantastic things before, turning out the F-80, America's first jet, in 141 days in World War II.

Bissell was a former isolationist with a convert's zeal for pressing the international designs of the United States. Gardner was a bold executive with a contempt for the Pentagon formula of decision by committee; a tough-minded industrialist, he indulged in no sentimentality about the U-2. He had come to the United States as a Welsh immigrant at the age of thirteen and by the time he was thirty he was general manager and executive vice-president of the General Tire and Rubber Company of California. At thirty-four he started his own research and development outfit, the Hycon Manufacturing Company.

Gardner had extensive experience in electronic intelligence, having secretly developed the air force's B57D reconnaissance bomber (the black watch), a variation on the Canberra, which the British used for aerial spying.

Gardner was an engineer with broad interests and did not believe that technical expertise was an American monopoly. He had a judicious respect for Russian scientists and technicians, and he figured the best way to judge how long the U-2 could fly safely over the Soviet Union was to calculate how long it would take the United States to develop a rocket that could knock down a Russian U-2. Gardner fully expected the Soviets to develop the means to counter the U-2 in a year or so.

Still, he and Bissell saw ample reason for taking the risk. Gardner was convinced the Russians were making significant advances in bombers and missiles, but he was finding it difficult to persuade his boss, Charles E. Wilson, the Secretary of Defense.

As the head of General Motors, Wilson had come to expect immediate practical results from his research men. He told the theoretical scientists and long-range planners in the Pentagon he had no interest in finding out if the moon was made of green cheese or why potatoes turned brown. He was also dubious about the claims of Soviet technology.

Every time Gardner would plead with him for more money, Wilson would reply: "You'll never convince me the Russians are nine feet tall."

If the U-2 were to bring back revealing pictures, Gardner reasoned, they might speak a thousand words to "Engine Charlie."

Even if the intelligence results were marginal, the U-2 might provoke the Russians into greater spending on their antiaircraft defenses, drawing off precious rubles from their offensive weaponry. The Soviets had an important military advantage in their secrecy. The location of defense installations in the United States was a matter of public record, easily double-checked by agents who could move more or less at will. In the Soviet Union, on the other hand, close to 40 percent of the country had been declared a "denied area." Travel by foreigners was ruthlessly policed.

Hundreds of U.S. planes were flying into Soviet air space, but even on daring raids with the RB-47 they could not penetrate more than a few hundred miles. And unbeknownst to the American public, scores of pilots were dying in crashes along the border.

At some point the Soviets would certainly be able to

detect the U-2. But if for a period they could do nothing about it, they might become convinced of the futility of their obsessive secrecy. They might think it preferable to accept an inspected arms control agreement.

These arguments were convincing to Talbott. He approved the program in December of 1954 and the money was provided by Wilfred J. McNeil, the Pentagon's comptroller. The initial outlay was small and Wilson went along with the order to build.

Knowledge of the operation was tightly restricted from the start. Only ten men were admitted to the secret— the three scientists, plus Bissell, Gardner, Talbott, McNeil, Wilson, Putt, and General Nathan F. Twining, Air Force Chief of Staff. Their names were listed on a yellow piece of paper. It was called a control sheet and it was then the only written document on the true nature of the U-2.

The top-secret control sheet gave Johnson the authority he needed. He returned to California and began to put the plane together in hundred-hour work weeks at his "Skunk Works," a maximum-security plant at Burbank, where he turned out the F-80 and F-104. All of the U-2's, originally called just "Kelly's plane," were hand-made at the Skunk Works at a cost of about $850,000 each.

To the men in Washington, Johnson's performance bordered on witchcraft. His central concept was to put a jet engine inside a glider, wrapping more airframe around the power plant than it was supposed to carry. Then the huge glider wings would support the whole weight of the aircraft and it could still be very light. It would not suffer the restrictions of ordinary jets, which cannot maintain extremely high altitudes because of their wing loadings. At the same time it could achieve an extraordinary range, flying for great distances, engine idling, conserving fuel.

The jet-engine manufacturers said it wouldn't work Airplanes are always underpowered, they argued, and at 70,000 feet the U-2 would have no thrust left. The military men, perhaps miffed because Johnson refused to forfeit altitude by allowing them to put a gun aboard, insisted the plane would come unglued.

But Bissell and Gardner were not to be frustrated by technical or bureaucratic objections. They trusted in Johnson's capacity to guess right, and he did. He guessed that a pressure suit could be built to prevent a pilot from exploding in the rarefied upper atmosphere if the cabin pressure failed. He guessed that a fuel could be developed that would not evaporate excessively at the U-2's extreme altitude.[3]

Johnson was confident he could eliminate weight and wind resistance by radically reducing the external parts of the plane. He did away with the landing gear by putting skids on the tips of the wings.[4]

He had no doubts about the camera. In August of 1955 the Air Force released photographs taken from 50,-000 feet. They clearly showed golf balls on a green.

Two efforts were made to conceal the U-2's role as a spy. It was thought at first that the plane could be designed so that radar could not detect it. But Johnson couldn't completely carry it off.

It was also thought that the plane might include an automatic destruction device. If the U-2 were to develop

[3] By 1960 MIL-F25524A had been perfected with a boiling point of 300 degrees Fahrenheit at sea level, twice that of normal fuel.
[4] The plane made a bicycle landing on the front and rear wheels attached to the body. At the end of the ground roll the pilot steered the plane onto a grassy area and let it plop over safely on one of the skids. With experience the U-2 pilots were to indulge in a little sport, keeping the wingtips aloft in the wind until the removable wheels were put in place. After an overflight, however, a pilot was too exhausted for games. He was often so weary that he had to be guided to a landing by radio signals.

trouble, it would explode automatically, destroying the plane and killing the pilot. It was quickly determined, however, that no practical mechanism could be devised. An automatic destructor might needlessly kill the pilot outside the Soviet Union. Or it could detonate in a situation where the pilot's ingenuity might enable him to get the plane working again.

Despite these difficulties Johnson was able to turn out the first model of the U-2 by August, 1955. Now Wilson would have to approve the larger funds involved in building limited quantities of the plane. Gardner and Johnson thought it might be a good idea to put on a little show for their reluctant boss.

Wilson was to be in Los Angeles during the Christmas holidays to serve as Grand Marshal of the Tournament of Roses. They decided to take him to the Skunk Works and "The Ranch," the test area at Watertown Strip.

The Secretary was skeptical of the sometimes elaborate claims of the plane makers. When he was criticized for failing to provide more money for an atomic airplane, Wilson would reply with a story. The A-plane reminded him, he would say, of the shitepoke, a heron that "flapped and flapped its wings but barely got off the ground."

The U-2 did, indeed, flap its wings at Watertown Strip that day, as it always would on takeoff. But it swooped high into the sky.

"It was like a lovely picture," one of the onlookers recalled. "You couldn't quite say how it was done, but the result was pleasing."

Wilson was put on the radio phone with a U-2 pilot who had been in the air for more than eight hours. His neck was bleeding from the pressure suit but he told the Secretary of Defense that he was prepared to stay aloft for another hour and a half. Wilson, who had been highly impressed by the nuts and bolts at Burbank, became a confirmed believer at Watertown Strip.

Johnson had proved that he could make the U-2 work as an airplane. Now it had to be made to work as a spy plane. This was essentially a human rather than a technical problem. The program, in the expression of those who ran it, had to be kept "black as a hat."

Over the objections of the Air Force, which felt the military could maintain tighter security, the operation was given to the C.I.A. Bissell was put in charge of it and he invoked the techniques of high espionage. Lie detector tests were administered to all involved in it and communications were restricted to word of mouth except for a bare minimum of documents. These were kept in top-secret safes and rarely removed from them.

The closest thing to a breach of security occurred when one of the handful of men in the C.I.A. who were privy to the facts dropped a U-2 document on the floor in closing his safe one night. It was a "hellish moment" for the offending official because an expert could have deduced the operation from the contents of the document. But a guard making his rounds spotted it on the floor and, reading no further than the classification marking at the top, haled the official back to the office.

Before the U-2 could start spying, President Eisenhower had to give his approval. And, according to the story he later related to intimates, he had misgivings.

As a military man he realized that a nation like an army had to have a battle plan. There had to be an avenue of retreat for both sides: if a U-2 were caught, the United States would need a graceful out and that would be possible only if there were a way for the Soviet Union to save face.

A White House meeting was arranged to brief the President on the program. It was attended by his leading advisers in the C.I.A. and the State and Defense Departments.

"If one of these planes is shot down," Eisenhower recalled saying, "this thing is going to be on my head. I'm going to catch hell. The world will be in a mess."

Advisers had replied that the Russians would have to suppress any incident. They could never run the risk of being humiliated by the revelation that their skies had been invaded repeatedly and they had not been able to do anything about it. But the President argued that the Russians would have no other choice. It would be the only way to stop the flights.

Those were the pros and cons of it as Eisenhower was later to relate them. Yet he was confronted by a difficult proposition: if he rejected the advice of his military and intelligence experts, he would, in effect, be depriving the nation of valuable, potentially matchless information. Then, too, the Russians were showing no sign of becoming more tractable.

Aware of the exciting possibilities of aerial reconnaissance, the President had offered an "Open Skies" proposal to the Soviets at a summit meeting in July of 1955 at Geneva. Nikolai Bulganin, the Soviet Premier, had expressed interest in the idea of mutual aerial inspection. But when the meeting broke up, Khrushchev, then First Secretary of the Communist Party, had turned to Eisenhower and said, "I don't agree with our chairman. This is not a good proposal. This is nothing but a great spy organization."

The President had learned who was the real boss of the Soviet Union. He had also learned there was little hope for Open Skies. Still, he persisted further, submitting his proposal in a more technical form to the United Nations Disarmament Commission the next month.

At that time, across from U.N. headquarters in New York, the Air Force staged an exhibition called "Mutual Inspection for Peace." It was a not-too-subtle demonstration of what the United States could do on its own. The principal display was a detailed film strip of an area 2,700 miles long and 490 miles wide taken from a plane between Los Angeles and New York in six hours and fifty-five minutes. It was seven years old.

Russian delegates observed the display with keen interest, but their government gave no indication of being prepared to accept Eisenhower's proposal. The President apparently realized his idea was getting nowhere. He decided to approve the plan for opening Soviet skies on our own.

Bissell set immediately to work creating the elaborate and deceptive machinery for running the U-2 program. The C.I.A. had no facilities, so the Air Force would have to take care of operations and logistics. But since military overtones were to be avoided, a "civilian" front would be required.

An approach was made to General James Doolittle, the leader of the first bomber raid on Tokyo during World War II. He was a member of the National Advisory Committee for Aeronautics and one of the original members of the President's Board of Consultants on Foreign Intelligence Activities.

Doolittle was asked to bring NACA into the operation as the cover for the U-2's espionage activities. He took the idea to Dryden, then Director of NACA, and Dryden accepted it immediately. NACA would be given access to the U-2 for high-altitude research, but its principal role would be to conceal the C.I.A.'s hand.

An April 30, 1956, NACA distributed a press release which said: "Tomorrow's jet transports will be flying air routes girdling the earth. This they will do at altitudes far higher than presently used except by a few military aircraft. The availability of a new type of airplane, the Lockheed U-2, makes possible obtaining the needed data (on gust-meteorological conditions) in an economical and expeditious manner . . .

"The program would not have been possible without the ability of American scientific effort to join forces . . . success of the program depends in large degree upon the logistical and technical support which the Air Weather Service of the USAF will be providing. USAF facilities will be used as the program gets under way, to enable gathering research information necessary to reflect accurately conditions in many parts of the world . . .

"The first data, covering conditions in the Rocky Mountain area, are being obtained from flights made from Watertown Strip, Nevada . . ."

Francis Gary Powers was to report to Watertown Strip the next month for his aerial spy training.

NACA's second release on the U-2, distributed on July 9, 1956, extended the cover to Europe by indicating "research flights" were also being conducted in England.

"Within recent weeks," the release stated, "preliminary data-gathering flights have been made from an air force base at Lakenheath, England, where the air service of the USAF is providing logistical and technical support."

The release also prepared the way for a further extension of the espionage operation overseas. "As the program continues," it added, "flights will be made in other parts of the world."

Further justification for the "weather flights" was advanced on March 27, 1957, when NACA issued a research memorandum on "preliminary measurements of atmospheric turbulence at high altitude as determined from acceleration measurements on Lockhead U-2 airplane."

The 14-page memorandum cited 17 flights conducted out of Lakenheath and Wiesbaden, Germany, between May and September, 1956, covering 22,000 flight miles.

NACA was already making preparations for the installation of instrument packages in the U-2 at overseas bases. It would conduct the operation itself for the first year while training military personnel, then turn the job over to the Air Force. The C.I.A. would prepare its own packages and neither NACA nor the Air Weather Service would ever see their innards.

But on the side, to justify the scientific portion of the program, NACA and the Air Weather Service would prepare joint packages at Wright-Patterson Air Force Base in Dayton, Ohio. These were used to gather "more precise information about clear air turbulence, convective clouds, wind shear, and the jet stream."

Over the next four years NACA pilots were to fly more than two hundred missions and over a quarter of a million miles in the U-2 in the interests of pure science. Four weighty scientific reports were to be published on the findings.

Only four people in the scientific organization were informed of the espionage operation.[5] Even so, a few NACA scientists down the line began to suspect something odd was going on.

[5] One of them was Dr. T. Keith Glennan, who was admitted to the secret in 1958 when he became the first director of the National Aeronautics and Space Administration, NACA's successor.

A plane for studying air turbulence ideally should have fixed wings, and the U-2's were flexible. The scientists began to express suspicions that the U-2 was being used as an atomic sampler to detect Soviet nuclear tests—and they were right, for NACA was also providing cover for atomic snooping.

Perhaps to satisfy the suspicions and preclude more perilous theorizing, the Defense Atomic Support Agency (DASA) began in 1958 to issue public reports on a High Altitude Sampling Program (HASP) [6] which employed the U-2.

Despite the best efforts at subterfuge, hints of the spy plane began to slip into the public prints as early as 1956.

On February 16, 1956, a U-2 crashed in Arizona when a fire started in the cockpit. The pilot was identified as Robert J. Everett, a Lockheed employee flying under NACA pilot number 357. He bailed out safely at 30,000 feet.

On June 1, 1956, a British aeronautical weekly, *Flight*, reported that a "mysterious stranger" had appeared over Lakenheath in Suffolk.

NACA was aroused enough by the disclosure to deem it wise to send its "cover" statements on the U-2 to *Flight*. "Perhaps the information they contain", a covering letter declared, "will assist in dispelling some of the mystery which appears to have enveloped the project."

On September 17, 1956, a U-2 crashed near Kaiserslautern, West Germany, killing the pilot, who was identified as Howard Carey, a Lockheed employee.

[6] After the Powers incident, the government announced the U-2 would continue to be used in the HASP project and in high-altitude weather research. Later it was announced that the U-2 would also be used to test equipment for missile detection satellites by training infrared gear on U.S. rocket firings. On January 2, 1962, a U-2 crashed near Picayune, Mississippi. The pilot, Captain Charles B. Stratton, said he bailed out when an electrical failure threw his automatic pilot out of control. He spent ten hours suspended in a cypress tree before he was rescued. Stratton had been in the same squadron with Powers at Turner Air Force Base, Georgia.

On April 4, 1957, a U-2 crashed in northwest Nevada, killing the pilot, who was identified as Robert L. Sieker, a Lockheed employee.

On April 14, 1957, the *Los Angeles Times* carried a story on the U-2 under the by-line of Marvin Miles, its knowledgeable aviation editor. He wrote that the U-2 was flying out of Europe and Japan under "top-secret classification."

"Even when they are on the ground at U.S. air bases," Miles said, "they are guarded day and night . . . Maybe the inspirational designations attributed to it by its crew, at least in one case, can give a clue to exceptional missions: Super-Snooper and St. Peter's Special."

In March, 1958, the *Model Airplane News* carried three simplified diagrams of the U-2 with the statement: "An unconfirmed rumor says that U-2's are flying across the Iron Curtain taking aerial photographs."

In May, 1958, in the first Russian press comment on the U-2, *Soviet Aviation,* a daily newspaper published by the Red Air Force, complained in a series of articles about "the black lady of espionage." It said the U-2 was flying out of Wiesbaden, West Germany, without any identification marks.

On July 10, 1958, the Strategic Air Command temporarily grounded its U-2's while investigating two fatal crashes within twenty-four hours. All told, five U-2 S.A.C. pilots were killed in 1957 and 1958.

In September, 1959, the Japanese magazine *Air Views* published a detailed account of a U-2 which made an emergency landing on a glider-club strip forty miles southwest of Tokyo.

"Undoubtedly the plane's activity is largely weather reconnaissance," wrote Eiichiro Sekigawa, the editor.

"Still it would be idle to think it is not being used for other reconnaissance while it goes about researching air conditions. Otherwise why was it necessary to threaten Japanese with guns to get them away from the crippled plane? And why did the plane have no identification marks? Why did the pilot have no identification marks on his clothes?"

. On November 24, 1959, the *New York Journal-American* carried a story on the U-2 by its aviation editor, George Carroll. It was a subtle piece saying not much of anything, yet saying a great deal. "No official agency has said so in so many words," Carroll wrote, "but you don't have to be a champion between-the-lines reader to get the pitch."

Still, few seemed to get the pitch even when a U-2 made a forced landing near Prince Albert, Canada, on March 15, 1960, just a month and a half before Powers' flight.

Despite the monumental security problem, Bissell was managing to keep his program a secret to the world and to most of the government. He did so by running a one-man operation.

Bissell maintained a tightly held priority targeting list containing the specific flights proposed, their exact routing, and their precise objectives. He was assisted in this by a group of Air Force technicians on loan to the C.I.A.

The list was continuously revised on the basis of informal conversations between Bissell and key men in the White House and the State and Defense Departments.

From time to time a series of flights—a very small number—would be selected from the list for completion during a short period, no more than a few weeks.

Not necessarily all in the series would go. If and when they did would depend on aircraft and pilot

E

readiness, and the weather. Cloud cover over the Soviet Union was bad for high-altitude photography except during short intervals. A series of flights might include an alternate plan for sending the missions on a different route if the weather looked bad along the original track.

After his word-of-mouth communications with the other agencies, Bissell would draw up his recommendations and bring them back for approval. If there were no objections at the State and Defense Departments, he would take his map to the White House and go over it with General Goodpaster. The White House and the other agencies did not so much approve the flights as hold a veto power over them.

Policy-makers in the State Department confessed they did not have the time or the expertise to make a judgment on the targets selected by the C.I.A. They had to rely on the technicians. Periodically, however, the White House would turn down a flight with the indication that the C.I.A. had not made a good enough case for it. On second thought, the technicians often agreed.

After a series had been accepted, word would be passed to the local commander in the field. Within the time limits set down by Washington, he would have wide discretion as to when to send the flights. He made his decision essentially on the basis of weather predictions. At any time a simple message from the C.I.A. could halt any flight. Whenever a mission had begun, the local commander would immediately notify the C.I.A. in Washington.

By 1960 the U-2 flights had become something of a milk run and the administrative procedures were routine. Hundreds of rank-and-file government workers were processing the U-2 pictures in the C.I.A.'s elaborate photo labs in Washington. And "consumers" were expanding all the time as the U-2's acquisitions became more varied.

The plane was bringing back significant intelligence on airfields, aircraft, missile testing and training, nuclear weapons storage, submarine production, atomic production and aircraft deployment.

The U-2 photos made Eisenhower shake his head in wonderment at the extraordinary clarity of the pictures. One of the greatest restraints on the program was the limited number of technicians who could adequately process the photos. Unprocessed U-2 film would often pile up for months and there seemed no sense in flying another mission until the results of the last were complete.

The U-2 was being used principally as a double-check on intelligence hints acquired in other ways—through American and Allied agents inside the Soviet Union or through the network of electronic listening equipment and radar.

The network tuned in repeatedly on the countdown conversations at the two Soviet missile test centers. And a mammoth radar near the Black Sea in Turkey tracked Russian IRBM and ICBM launchings starting in 1955. When it had been determined that something interesting might be visible, the U-2 was sent in to take a picture of it.

At one point a U-2 was sent over China to check a report that the Peking regime had its first ballistic missile upright on a pad ready for firing. It turned out to be a tall medieval tower.

Because of the extensive information it was bringing back on military installations, the U-2 inevitably became involved in the "bomber gap" and "missile gap" controversies of the 1950's.

The Democrats, supported by an influential and vocal

wing of the Air Force, were charging that the Eisenhower Administration was permitting the Soviet Union to surpass the United States in bomber and missile strength.

In the spring of 1957, Senator Stuart Symington, the Missouri Democrat, complained that the official intelligence estimates of Soviet bomber strength had been radically downgraded in the previous year.

Allen Dulles, who considered the U-2 the most useful intelligence tool of the cold war, promptly replied in a letter: "The estimate of Soviet heavy bomber strength as of April 1, 1956, which was given in my testimony before your subcommittee, was largely based on an estimated build-up rate which rested upon earlier evidence. Subsequent to my testimony before your committee in April, 1956, the intelligence community acquired new and better evidence on Soviet heavy-bomber production and strength in operational units and we undertook a complete review of our estimates on this subject [which] revised downwards the estimated total production on Bisons (the Russian equivalent of the B-52) . . ."

The U-2 had been flying over Red Air Force bases for a year now, providing the "new and better evidence." The U-2 brought back indications that Soviet technology was considerably further advanced than had been thought, but it produced no indication that the Russians were using their skill to build large numbers of weapons. Dulles was hinting in his letter that the U-2 could find no evidence that the Soviets had embarked on a massive bomber production program as Symington and others had warned.

Similarly, at the height of the "missile gap" furor near the end of the decade, those who ran the U-2 program reported the plane was able to locate only two ICBM sites in the Soviet Union, both of them test centers.

Symington was to learn of the exact source of Dulles' "evidence" on Christmas Eve of 1959 while traveling through the Middle East with Fowler Hamilton, a fellow Missourian who was to become Director of the Agency for International Development in the Kennedy Administration. During a briefing by an Air Force officer at Adana,[7] the two men were shown a chart listing the 10-10 detachment and its commander, Colonel Shelton.

"What's that one?" Symington asked.

"We don't talk about that one," the briefing officer replied.

"What do they do?" Symington persisted.

"We don't know," the briefing officer protested, explaining that it was a civilian project run by NASA.

"Then why is a colonel running it?" Symington demanded.

The briefing officer would still offer no explanation. Symington gave him ten minutes to produce Shelton himself. The colonel appeared but refused to talk in the presence of Hamilton, who later was briefly the leading candidate to succeed Dulles as head of the C.I.A.

Alone with Shelton, Symington pointed out that he himself was a former Secretary of the Air Force and had access to top-secret information as a member of the Senate Armed Services Committee. Shelton still refused to reveal his mission.

Symington had learned of the supersecret U-2 operation in a general way through unofficial channels. Now he realized he was face to face with it. He left, impressed with the high and unbending sense of security of the commander of the 10-10 detachment.

[7] In addition to Turkey and Pakistan, the U-2 was also flying out of Japan, Formosa, Okinawa, the Philippines, Alaska, West Germany, and England.

►5
►
►

"What Happens
If You're Caught?"

BARBARA POWERS AWOKE IN
her trailer on the base at Incirlik at 5:00 A.M. Monday,
May 2, to the sound of pounding on her front door. It was
still dark and the mountains to the north were only dim
shapes on the horizon.

Sleepily, she went to the door. Several of her husband's friends were there. The thought passed through
her mind that this was "just another wake-up party." They
were sometimes held for amusement by the pilots and
wives of the isolated and closely knit 10-10 detachment.

"This had better be good," Barbara told the group at
the door.

"Barbara, we have some bad news," one of the men
replied unsmilingly. "Gary is missing. We have search
planes out but they haven't found him yet."

What followed was later hazy in her mind. "The next thing I remember is the base doctor giving me shots. I don't know how many I had. I just don't ever want to have another." For the next few days she remained under heavy sedation, awaiting word of Gary's fate.

At the Municipal Palace in Istanbul, the NATO foreign ministers met while Turkish troops stood warily on guard outside.

Herter was at the conference table in the palace when Livingston Merchant, Under Secretary of State for Political Affairs, handed him a slip of paper. The message had been relayed by a C.I.A. representative at Ankara. It referred simply to a missing plane; but because the slip of paper bore C.I.A. markings, the Secretary of State immediately realized that a U-2 was down.

At Adana, Yusuf Ayhan, a local newsman who spoke Turkish and Arabic but no English, thought he was onto an interesting story. Ayhan regularly checked with the public information office at the Incirlik base for news. He had on this day picked up an interesting tip, and he was able to confirm it at the base.

The Turkish newsman was the first to receive, and write, the cover story plotted out with slide rules by the men at the C.I.A. meeting in Washington the previous day.

Ayhan earned extra money as a stringer, or part-time correspondent, for *Yeni Istanbul* (New Istanbul), and he thought the story he had stumbled on was good enough to file to Istanbul for the next day's paper.

"An American plane of the U-2 meteorological reconnaissance type, which is well known for its excellent performance, and was based at Incirlik near Adana, was reported missing on Sunday," Ayhan wrote. "The U-2 plane, which flies at an altitude over 10,000 meters, thereby approaching the atmosphere to investigate the reasons behind changes in weather conditions, had sent its last message on Sunday, when the pilot reported a breakdown of his oxygen equipment. No further news was received from the plane after that."

But Ayhan, like any good newsman, had sources of his own. He had a feeling, he wrote, that the plane might have been shot down by "Russian fighters." The Air Force did not agree with Ayhan's theory, for the story added: "A press office bulletin issued at 4:00 P.M. said it is possible that the plane in question made a forced landing in the vicinity of Lake Van. It is reported that other planes which took off from Tripoli to search for the missing plane have failed to garner any information."

Not much, perhaps, but Adana was a slow news town, and Ayhan was confident that his file to the Istanbul paper would be printed, which also meant that he, Yusuf Ayhan, would be paid.

At 3:30 P.M., Harry Press's telephone rang.

Press, a bespectacled, cautious bureaucrat with a cherubic face, was in his office at 1512 H Street one block from the White House.

He was Chief, Loads and Structures Division, NASA. He was also one of the four men at NASA who knew that the U-2 was photographing military targets in the Soviet Union under NASA cover. For two years, he had run NASA's overt end of the program from Langley Field.

This day, the caller was Major James Smith, at the Air Force Air Weather Service headquarters, Scott Air Force Base, Belleville, Illinois. Major Smith was the U-2

project officer there and Press's regular contact with the
Air Force. He told Press essentially the same cover story
that Yusuf Ayhan had picked up in Adana several hours
earlier.

Under the cover arrangements, the "Second Weather
Observational Squadron (Provisional)" at Adana reported
to the Second Weather Wing, Wiesbaden, Germany. The
wing in turn reported to A.W.S. headquarters at Scott.

Had Press known of the Sunday C.I.A. meeting—
which he did not—he might have deduced that the message he received had gone out from Washington to Adana,
to Wiesbaden, to Illinois, and then to him on H Street. It
had gone halfway around the globe and back again to
travel a few blocks in downtown Washington.

Press thanked Major Smith and passed on the news
to Dryden and Walter T. Bonney, NASA's director of public information. He was not surprised that they already
seemed to know.

Meanwhile a powerful but almost unknown agency,
the United States Intelligence Board, moved quietly into
the behind-the-scenes decision-making on the U-2. Its
chairman was Allen Dulles, and it included the heads of
the intelligence branches of the armed services, and a
representative of the National Security Agency, which en-
gages in ultrasecret cryptography and electronic espionage. Cumming was the State Department's man on the
board.

He was increasingly worried over the missing U-2 and
its pilot. He wanted to bring a widening circle of officials
into the consultations, particularly Charles E. "Chip"
Bohlen.

Although Bohlen, former Ambassador to Moscow, was
now the State Department's top Soviet expert, he was not

among those who officially knew of the U-2 flights. Each
new person let in on the secret had to be cleared by the
White House. On Monday, May 2, Cumming sought and
obtained clearance to tell Bohlen what was going on.[1]

In Moscow, Marshal Vershinin had a small request to
make of the Pentagon. His message was relayed to Washington. The previous Friday, April 29, Vershinin had accepted an invitation to visit America with nine fellow
Soviet air officers. It was to be in return for a visit to the
Soviet Union in 1956 of a delegation headed by Twining,
who four years later had become chairman of the Joint
Chiefs of Staff. Vershinin wondered whether the announcement of his trip to the United States might be delayed forty-eight hours.

Zeyyat Goren, United Press International manager
for Turkey, was covering the NATO meeting at Istanbul
May 3 when he received a telephone call from Adan Tahir,
a reporter on the staff of *Hurriyet*, an Istanbul newspaper.
Tahir was paid by Goren for news tips. He called to tell
the UPI bureau chief that a weather plane was missing
from Incirlik. Goren telephoned the base and was put
through to a duty sergeant in the press office.

The Air Force sergeant confirmed the story; the plane,
he said, had been lost "near the Persian border." There had
been oxygen trouble, and a search was in progress by three
C-54 planes from Wheelus Air Force Base, Libya. Goren
was interested; he recalled the crash of the C-130 in the
same area in 1958, and was well aware that the "Persian

---

[1] Bohlen had just returned from a trip to Moscow; he landed in Boston
April 29, spent the weekend there, and did not arrive in Washington until
late Monday.

border" adjoined the border of Soviet Armenia. The Air Force sergeant did not seem to know the name of the U-2 pilot.

Goren cabled the story to UPI in New York; on East Forty-second Street in Manhattan, Bill Fox, the day cable editor, put it on the A wire for dispatch to all UPI subscribers throughout North America.

The story did not find its way into many papers. In the capital that evening, the *Washington Post* ran the three-inch item on page one. It was dropped in the final street edition to make room for a baseball headline: "NATS DEFEAT TRIBE 7–6 ON GREEN'S HIT IN 9TH."

Like a very small fish swimming from a river into the sea, the story of the U-2 had entered the flow of the day's news, almost unnoticed.

The President had left Washington at 8:00 A.M., May 3, and flown to Fort Benning, Georgia, to watch an exhibition of Army firepower. He gave a short speech praising the "wonderful weapons," then returned to Washington by plane.

Something else happened in the capital, although it seemed like a small thing at the time. A long list of possible questions and suggested answers had been prepared in advance by C.I.A. to serve as guidelines for NASA if and when a U-2 was downed over Russia and newsmen queried the space agency. The list was supposed to have been cleared with the State Department, but it hadn't been. Instead, it went directly to NASA.[2]

---

2 A similar list was prepared for the Air Force. Expected questions and canned answers on the list were designed to mislead newsmen who telephoned asking about the missing "weather" plane. The document read, in part:

At the space agency, Harry Press was unhappy.

He had an unpleasant duty to perform. Dryden had given him the name of Francis Gary Powers and had assigned him the task of telling the family that the pilot was missing on a weather flight over Turkey.

Informed that Powers' mother had a heart condition, Press decided to notify two of Powers' sisters living near Washington. He first telephoned William Edward Hileman, who was in the newspaper delivery business and married to Powers' twenty-four-year-old sister, Jessica. The Hilemans lived in Glass Manor, Maryland. Jessica worked in Washington, at the Hartford Accident and Indemnity Co.

Press reached Hileman at work, said he had bad news for his wife and would like them both to go home and wait for him there.

A group of men arrived at the Hileman house in Glass Manor soon afterwards, including Press, an agent of the C.I.A., and a man who said he was a Lockheed official.

Mrs. Hileman was badly shaken at the news. She suggested they all go to nearby Falls Church, Virginia, to notify her sister Janice, wife of Veril W. Melvin, an electrician. The group drove across the Potomac to Virginia and the same emotional scene was repeated at the Melvin home.

Both sisters were immensely proud of their brother. He was the big success in the family.

Q. Do these missions include photo reconnaissance of the Soviet Union?

A. Negative.

Q. Have Strategic Air Command U-2's operated outside the United States?

A. Yes, but never out of the Western Hemisphere.

Q. Does this aircraft have any tactical or strategic capabilities?

A. None whatsoever, as it was not designed for such purposes.

Janice and Jessica had planned to go to Pound for the weekend to visit their parents; now they decided to leave sooner.

The mines are pretty well worked out around Norton, Virginia, fifteen miles due south of Pound. A community of 5,000 persons, it was still prosperous only because of the demand for coke, produced in the huge, smoking ovens on the hillsides and shipped to the Great Lakes for steel-making.

A few doors down Seventh Street, just off Norton's broad main thoroughfare, the sign on the window of the small shop at No. 15 read "Better Shoe Repairing." Underneath appeared the single word: "Powers."

The fifty-five-year-old heavy-set man behind the counter was chain-smoking Pall Malls. He worked over the shoes with strong hands, stained from leather, shoe polish, and tobacco, fingernails dirty. They were hands that had worked hard from boyhood.

Into Oliver's shoe shop at 4:00 P.M. this afternoon walked two men. One identified himself as "from Lockheed, in Burbank, California." The other said he was from the space agency in Washington. As gently as they could, they told Oliver his boy was missing on a weather flight in northern Turkey. The two men said that planes had been searching for three days, but had found no trace of him.

In Moscow, the Soviet Union announced the award of the Lenin Peace Prize to Cleveland industrialist Cyrus Eaton. Khrushchev opened a Czechoslovak trade exhibit in Sokolniki Park and appeared in high good humor. He picked up a rifle at a shooting gallery and made a bull's-eye on the first shot.

In Paris, the chestnut trees along the Champs Elysées were in bloom and preparations for the summit conference were moving forward. Children were laughing at a special summit puppet show. The puppets depicted President De Gaulle, Prime Minister Macmillan, Eisenhower, and Khrushchev.

Above them fluttered the dove of peace.

Wednesday, May 4, was the seventh day since Powers had left Adana. Now, Colonel Shelton told Barbara to go back to the United States as soon as possible. Shelton explained that when her husband was found he would be taken immediately to the United States for a medical examination. She would see him sooner, the colonel argued, by going home rather than by staying.

This did not seem to make much sense to Barbara. She had her first premonition that something very odd was happening. Nevertheless she followed her instructions, packed, and began making arrangements for the long trip home to Milledgeville.

During the afternoon, the NATO meeting ended at Istanbul. Herter and his party flew to Athens, where he was scheduled to spend two nights and dine with King Paul.

Francis Powers' grandfather had been born when Ulysses S. Grant was President. James Powers was ninety now, a tall figure with a white beard, a floppy felt hat and a cane he used not only to walk with, but to poke good-naturedly at anyone within reach. His memory was failing a bit, and all the members of the family treated the old man gently as he wandered about the house amidst his numerous grandchildren.

Ida Powers, a gentle, soft-voiced woman, had not been in the best of health since her heart attack. The wrinkles in her thin, lined face made her look older than her fifty-four years. Wearing a flower-print apron, she was busy in her kitchen, just off the small living room, when Oliver walked into their home, accompanied by Jessica.

She was surprised, because her daughter was not due to arrive for another two days, but happy, too, since there would now be a fine family reunion, minus Francis, of course. Three other daughters lived only a few yards down the dirt road winding through the lonely hollow.

Jean, the oldest girl, a lovely brunette, was married to Jack Goff, who owned a shoe shop in Pound and drove a school bus. Joan, a friendly, dark-haired woman, close to her brother Francis, was the wife of Walton Meade, the Pound postman, and Joyce, the blond baby of the family, was married to Roy Stallard, a farmer.

Ida Powers asked Jessica how it was she had arrived two days early. "I just took a notion to come," Jessica replied. Ida could tell by their faces that something was very wrong. She insisted they tell her. Finally they broke the news. Francis was missing somewhere in Turkey. Ida Powers sat down and started to cry.

In Moscow, the Russians finally announced Marshal Vershinin's visit to America; he would arrive May 14 at Washington National Airport. Khrushchev, in an expansive mood at a Czech Embassy reception, dropped a tidbit: the Soviet Union's rocket forces had been elevated to a separate branch of the armed services and placed under the command of Marshal Mitrofan Ivanovich Nedelin.

Tomorrow, Khrushchev told the Western and Eastern diplomats at the reception, he would go before the Supreme Soviet, the Russian parliament. He promised that his speech would be interesting.

Cumming was to receive an honorary key at the University of Virginia the next day. He left Washington on May 4 and drove south toward his alma mater at Charlottesville.

At the White House the President breakfasted with Republican Congressional leaders, signed a wheat agreement with India and went out to the Burning Tree Club for a round of golf.

But the President's press secretary, James C. Hagerty, that day learned a disquieting piece of news. The "weather" plane down in Turkey was actually a U-2 missing over Russia.

At the Commodore Hotel in New York just after the 1952 election, the press secretary had had a long talk with Eisenhower. They agreed that Hagerty would be told of security secrets only on a "need to know" basis. For a long time, therefore, Hagerty had not known about the spy flights.

But about six months before, in the fall of 1959, the President and Hagerty were riding together in an automobile on one of Eisenhower's weekend trips. On such occasions the two men often talked intimately and at length, almost like father and son.

In the midst of one of these rambling conversations, Eisenhower turned to Hagerty suddenly and revealed that United States planes were flying over the Soviet Union.

We're getting some information back from Russia, Jim, the President had said.

But the President made it plain he was worried about the overflights. He had often asked the C.I.A.: What happens if you're caught?

Every time he did so, the C.I.A. responded: It hasn't happened yet.

► **6**

Taking the Minnow

IT WAS THE FIFTH OF MAY. In the Great Hall of the great Kremlin Palace, the 1,300 delegates to the Supreme Soviet were already in their benches.

A spectators' balcony in the back of the long white chamber sloped down to a press box on the right rear side. The diplomatic corps had an excellent view from boxes along the right wall.

Seated in one of them, Ambassador Thompson had an uneasy feeling. He had been placed in a choice position, a front box, to which he was not entitled by protocol. There was, Thompson reflected, something funny about it.

At the front of the Great Hall, a nine-foot white statue of Lenin, his right arm raised, towered over the delegates.

At 10:00 A.M., Khrushchev mounted the rostrum in front
of the statue, put on his gold-rimmed glasses and launched
into a marathon speech. It was 3:00 A.M. in Washington
as he began.

Behind Khrushchev sat the stony-faced members of
the Presidium, among them Malinovsky.

Khrushchev, wearing three medals on his dark suit,
unfolded a new tax and currency program: personal income taxes would gradually be abolished by 1965; the
ruble would be pegged at ten times its present value; new
kopeks were to be minted.

He spoke, pessimistically, of the coming summit conference. The recent speeches of Nixon, Herter, and Dillon
"are far from inspiring hope for a favorable outcome of the
talks opening May 16." He doubted that the West really
wanted "concrete solutions." Why did the West not understand the Soviet Union's peaceful desire to sign a peace
treaty with the "two German states"? He regretted Eisenhower's intention to have Nixon represent him at the summit conference if he had to leave Paris before it was over.[1]
Nixon, he said, was not interested in ending the cold war.
He had met Nixon, and if Nixon were at the summit it
would be like "letting a goat watch over the cabbage
patch."

It was toward the very end of his three-and-a-half-
hour speech that Khrushchev dropped the bombshell.

Early on the morning of May Day, he declared, "at
5:36 A.M. Moscow time, an American plane crossed our
border and continued its flight into Soviet territory. The
Minister of Defense immediately notified the government
of this aggressive act. The government told him: the ag-

---

[1] Eisenhower had announced April 26 that he might send Nixon to Paris if
"domestic" requirements necessitated his own return to Washington.

gressor knows what to expect when he invades foreign
territory. If he goes unpunished he will commit new provo-
cations. The thing to do, therefore, is to act—shoot down
the plane. These instructions were carried out, the plane
was shot down."

The official Russian translation, which includes audience reaction, noted: "(Stormy, prolonged applause. Shouts
of 'Quite Right!' 'Shame on the aggressor.')"

"The first investigation," Khrushchev continued, "has
shown that the plane belonged to the United States, though
it had no identification insignia—they had been painted
over. (Shouts of indignation. 'How is this to be reconciled
with Eisenhower's pious speeches? That is outright ban-
ditism!')"

Another United States plane had invaded Soviet air
space on April 9, Khrushchev declared, but the Kremlin
decided not to make any useless official protest. Instead,
"we strictly warned our military commanders, especially
those directly responsible for the nation's antiaircraft defense, that they must act resolutely and not allow unpunished invasion of our air space by foreign planes. (Shouts
of 'Quite right!' Prolonged applause.)"

"Just imagine what would have happened if a Soviet
aircraft were to appear, say over New York, Chicago or Detroit . . . How would the United States react? United
States officials have repeatedly declared that they keep
A-bomb and H-bomb planes on the alert, and that with
the approach of a foreign aircraft they would take off and
head for their designated bombing targets. That would
mean the outbreak of war.

". . . Nobody doubts that we have what is needed to
retaliate."

Countries that provide bases for such flights "are playing with fire. Retaliatory blows will be dealt these countries, too." Russia would protest to the U.N.

He was, Khrushchev said, about to go to Paris to meet Eisenhower, and now the U.S. Air Force had committed an aggressive act. Khrushchev looked up at the box where Thompson sat, and asked: "What is this, May Day greetings? (Commotion.)"

The United States was seeking to "torpedo" the summit, he charged.

"The question then arises: Who sent this aircraft across the Soviet Frontier? Was it dispatched with the approval of the commander-in-chief of the United States armed forces, a post, as we know, held by the President? Or was this aggressive act undertaken by the Pentagon militarists without the President's knowledge? If acts of this kind are undertaken by the American militarists at their own discretion, that should arouse the deepest concern of world public opinion."

Khrushchev's voice became vibrant and emotional as he attacked the "bandit flight," adding that "attempts to force us to bend the knee and bow the head will have no effect whatsoever. . . . It is not for nothing that we have the saying: 'He who comes with the sword shall perish by the sword.' (Applause.)"

He had not forgotten his friendly talks with Eisenhower at Camp David, but the Soviet Union was a "great power," it had placed the first Sputnik in the sky and it was not to be intimidated.

"Under the banner of Lenin, under the leadership of the Communist Party, to new victories in the construction of communism! (Stormy and prolonged applause. All rise.)"

In the rear of the Great Hall, Western reporters rushed for the telephones.

It was just after dawn in Washington.

At 7:00 A.M., all members of the National Security Council, the top strategy board of the United States government, were notified by telephone to report immediately to various predesignated helicopter pads for evacuation from the capital.

As part of a three-day nationwide "Operation Alert 1960" Civil Defense exercise, the N.S.C. would meet with the President at the "Crow's Nest," a highly secret, partly underground dispersal headquarters located in the mountains within a sixty-mile radius of Washington.

From homes around the capital, in nearby Virginia and Maryland, men carrying attaché cases climbed into waiting limousines and sped to takeoff points. Secretary of Defense Gates left from a Navy installation at Massachusetts and Nebraska Avenues. The President took off by helicopter from the White House at 7:30 A.M., unaware, like the other members of the N.S.C., of Khrushchev's speech.

At 7:36 A.M., the Washington bureau of UPI received an urgent message from New York:

WA

REUTERS SAYING KHRUSHCHEV SED IN SPEECH TDAY TT U.S. PLANE SHOT DOWN SUNDAY FR VIOLATING SOVIET AIR SPACE. SUG CK DEF DEPT. SAP.

NXD JL736A5/5

New York was suggesting that Washington check the Department of Defense as soon as possible (SAP) on the British wire service report.

At about the same moment, Gates was receiving the

news of Khrushchev's speech by military radio as his helicopter droned toward the mountainside Civil Defense
hideaway.

At the White House, Hagerty, who did not go to the
N.S.C. meeting, answered a call from the UPI Washington
bureau, three blocks away in the National Press Building.
Hagerty told the press association he was not aware that
an American plane had been shot down inside the Soviet
Union; he had not heard about Khrushchev's speech.

UPI managed to rouse Herbert Schon, a Department
of Defense spokesman, at his home, but he said he knew
nothing of any American plane down in Russia.

"It strikes me cold," Schon told UPI.

All of this took a few minutes, and New York was
getting impatient. At 7:44 A.M., eight minutes after the
first message, another crackled across the closed wire from
UPI in Manhattan to Washington:

WA

     ND SAP REACTION KHRUSHCHEV STTMNT TT U.S.
PLANE SHOT DOWN SOV TERRITORY.

NXD JH744A

The wire service began to move copy to satisfy the
edgy New York editor. Soon afterward, Hagerty placed a
call to the N.S.C. meeting. He reached Goodpaster, who
informed him that the President was already in the N.S.C.
meeting.

Hagerty told Goodpaster he would await instructions
from the President. A few moments later Goodpaster called
Hagerty back and told him there would be a meeting on
the U-2 after the N.S.C. meeting; he would either call Hag-

erty back afterwards and inform him of the results, or return directly to the White House by helicopter and do so
then.

In Athens, Ellis O. Briggs, the United States Ambassador to Greece, was holding a reception for the Secretary
of State. Diplomats moved easily about the room, chatting and sipping drinks. Into this scene walked Clary
Thompson, an official of the United States Information
Agency. In his hand were ticker reports of the Khrushchev
speech. He sought out Andrew Berding, the Assistant Secretary of State for Public Affairs, and gave him the wire
copy. Berding, who knew nothing of the U-2 operation,
discreetly whispered the news to Herter. The reception
continued.

Cumming, driving back from the University of Vir-
ginia early in the morning, was nearing Culpepper on
U.S. Route 29 when he idly flipped on his car radio.
". . . Moscow," the announcer intoned, "Premier
Khrushchev said today the Soviet Union shot down an
American plane Sunday inside Soviet territory . . ."
Cumming nearly drove into a ditch.
He regained control of the car, screeched to a stop at
the first gas station and called his office at the State De-
partment from a public phone booth. He reached his as-
sistant, J. Lampton Berry, who quickly filled him in on
details of the Khrushchev speech.

The N.S.C. meeting in the war room of the Civil Defense headquarters had ended, and a select few of the
sixteen officials who had attended it moved into a smaller
room next door. The setting was informal—sofas, chairs,

but no table. Gathered here were six of the most powerful
men in America:

Douglas Dillon, former board chairman of the Wall
Street banking firm of Dillon, Read & Co., which his father
had founded, and owner of Château Haut-Brion, in France,
which produced one of the five finest clarets in the world.
With Herter still away, Dillon was running the State Department.

Thomas Gates, the Philadelphia financier, a big, bluff,
handsome man, the boss of the awesome armed might of
the United States.

Allen Dulles, wartime head of the Office of Strategic
Services in Switzerland, inevitably referred to as the "master spy" by the Sunday supplements, for seven years now
director of the C.I.A.

Gordon Gray, scion of a North Carolina tobacco and
publishing family, special assistant to the President for
national security.

General Goodpaster, a tall, graying West Pointer with
a Ph.D. from Princeton, the President's right arm and his
link with the Pentagon and the shadowy intelligence world.

The meeting was brief. The President attended it but
left abruptly to keep an 11:30 A.M. appointment with
Twining. Goodpaster had to dash to make the helicopter
back to the White House with the President. He had no
chance to telephone Hagerty.

During the short meeting inside the little room in the
mountainside, Dillon and most of the others felt that a
statement would have to be made, that there would have
to be some reaction to Khrushchev's charges.

The consensus was that there could be no turning
back, no admission of espionage. Traditionally, all nations
spy, but none admit it. The decision was reached to keep

on telling the cover story; all statements would be made by the State Department.

But Gates was troubled. He warned that the prestige of the Presidency should not be involved in "an international lie." He suggested that if Khrushchev had the physical evidence, the President of the United States might have to admit the truth.

Gates was overruled. The decision was to continue to lie. The State Department would do the lying.

Dulles concurred in this decision. With his white mustache, white hair, and rimless glasses, he looked more the part of a grandfather than a spy chief. His two favorite forms of relaxation were pipe-smoking and bass-fishing.

The C.I.A. director regarded bass-fishing as an art. You had to use minnows as bait, he would say. Then you must wait as the bass takes the minnow by the tail and turns it around in his mouth. Only then do you strike, so that the hook goes into the upper lip.

The President, the Director of Central Intelligence, the Secretary of Defense, the Acting Secretary of State, and the chairman of the N.S.C. did not know it, but they had just taken the minnow, and were now slowly turning it in their mouths.

In his office, Hagerty was besieged all morning by newsmen seeking comment on the sensational charge by Khrushchev. Since he had no instructions as yet from Goodpaster, Hagerty could say nothing.

The President and Goodpaster landed at the White House at 11:24 A.M.

At 12:05 P.M., Hagerty called in newsmen and announced:

"At the direction of the President, a complete inquiry

is being made. The results of this inquiry, the facts as developed, will be made public by the National Aeronautics and Space Administration and the Department of State."

It was the first time anyone had mentioned a statement by NASA. The officials at the mountainside conference had decided that the State Department, and only the State Department, would make any comment. Hagerty may have erred; or he may have acted on instructions from Goodpaster—accounts conflict.

But it was clear that somewhere between the mountainside meeting and the White House, there was a serious breakdown in communication. It was the initial error in a day of monumental confusion.

Hagerty indicated that the reporters would do well to get right over to NASA. N.B.C.'s Ray Scherer and *Newsweek's* Charles Roberts ran across Lafayette Park from the White House and burst into Bonney's office on H Street.

"Where's the statement?" asked Scherer.

Two secretaries looked at the huffing and puffing newsmen in utter astonishment. "What statement?" they caroled in unison.

"The statement that Jim Hagerty said you were going to put out," replied Scherer.

No one had told NASA's press chief that he was to put out a statement. Bonney retreated to his inner office and immediately called Hagerty. A few moments later, he announced he would have a statement after all, at 1:30 P.M.

The newsmen went out for a quick lunch.

During the morning, officials of C.I.A. and the State Department were meeting to work out the text of a statement to be issued by Lincoln White, department spokesman. The statement was released at 12:45 P.M. White, who

did not know that the U-2 was a spy plane, apologized to
the mob of reporters for being late for his noon briefing,
then declared:

"The Department of State has been informed by
NASA that as announced May 3 an unarmed plane, a U-2
weather research plane based at Adana, Turkey, piloted
by a civilian, has been missing since May 1. During the
flight of this plane, the pilot reported difficulty with his
oxygen equipment. Mr. Khrushchev announced that a U.S.
plane has been shot down over the U.S.S.R. on that date.
It may be that this is the missing plane. It is entirely possible that having a failure in the oxygen equipment, which
could result in the pilot losing consciousness, the plane
continued on automatic pilot for a considerable distance
and accidentally violated Soviet air space. The United
States is taking this matter up with the Soviet government, with particular reference to the fate of the pilot."

Q. Linc, how do you know the plane was having difficulty?

A. He reported it.

Q. He reported it by radio?

A. That is right.

Q. At what time did he give his position?

A. In the Lake Van area.

Q. Was his course such at this time that if continued
it might have taken him over to the Soviet Union?

A. John [Hightower, AP], I don't have those details.

Pressed for the name of the pilot, White told the newsmen that he knew it, but that the pilot's mother had a
cardiac condition; he hoped he could withhold the name
until the doctor had had a chance to break the news to the
mother.

It was now past 1:00 P.M. A bulletin clattered across the UPI wire:

UPI 89

    (PLANE)

THE STATE DEPARTMENT SAID TODAY THAT AN AMERICAN PLANE MAY HAVE DRIFTED ACROSS THE RUSSIAN BORDER LAST SUNDAY AS A RESULT OF THE PILOT BECOMING UNCONSCIOUS FROM LACK OF OXYGEN.

    5/5—MJ108P

In a more leisurely era, Dolley Madison lived in the house that was now NASA headquarters. There, while White was meeting newsmen at the State Department, Bonney spent an agonizing three-quarters of an hour. By now, it was clear to the NASA press chief that, in the line of official duty, he was going to have to go out and lie convincingly to the newsmen who had trusted him.

Bonney had never intended to go to work for the government in the first place. An ex-aviation reporter for the Springfield (Mass.) *Republican,* he had joined Bell Aircraft in Buffalo in 1941, but left because the climate affected his daughter's health. With his aviation background, he found quiet work in Washington, as information director of the obscure NACA. He had not expected it to lead to this.

From the start, Bonney had known the U-2 was an espionage plane. Dryden considered it essential that one man in the public information division know the full details of the program. Bonney was tapped.

Between May 1 and 5, both Dryden and Bonney had

been in direct contact with C.I.A., going over the list of questions and false answers that had been sent to the space agency without clearance by the State Department. C.I.A. instructed NASA to answer newsmen's questions and provide the cover answers.

On this Thursday, nobody had bothered to inform NASA of the decision made after the N.S.C. meeting that only the State Department would speak for the government. Hagerty had referred reporters to NASA; they were on Bonney's doorstep demanding information. Bonney, after calling Hagerty, consulted with Dryden. It was decided to take the C.I.A. question-and-answer sheet and meld it into one statement for the press. It would be better, Dryden felt, than to engage in a "free-for-all" with the reporters.

Bonney closeted himself in his office with the C.I.A. guidelines, personally typed up a statement in rough form and gave it to a secretary. She smoothed out the language as she retyped it on a multilith mat. It was then run off on machines and rushed to the NASA auditorium next door, where newsmen were already beginning to gather.

The United States government was now about to make one of the most critical statements of the cold war. It had been hastily drafted, and edited by a secretary. It had not been cleared with the State Department, the C.I.A. or the White House. It had not been seen by either Herter, Dulles, or the President.

Bonney walked into the NASA auditorium and began reading from a four-page, double-spaced "Memo to the Press," NASA release No. 60–193. Like a Bach fugue, it richly orchestrated the theme originally stated in the cover story issued at Adana by the Air Force sergeant, and repeated by Lincoln White.

A U-2 research plane, used to study "gust-meteorological conditions," had been missing since Sunday, after
the pilot reported oxygen trouble over Lake Van. Then
Bonney added new details; he reeled off the triangular
flight plan of the U-2 plotted at Sunday's C.I.A. meeting—
northeast to the Lake Van beacon, northwest to the Trebizond beacon, southwest to Antalya, and east to Adana,
1,400 nautical miles, estimated flight time, 3 hours 45 minutes. The pilot was last heard from on a northeasterly
course. Like all U-2 pilots, he was employed by Lockheed.
The U-2 could fly for as much as four hours at altitudes of
"up to 55,000 feet." The U-2's instruments, the reporters
were told, would permit "more precise information about
clear air turbulence, convective clouds, windshear, the jet
stream and typhoons," not to mention "cosmic rays . . .
ozone and water vapor." There followed a long list of technical equipment carried by the plane to measure temperature, humidity, and air speed.

Why, a reporter wanted to know, was the weather
plane flying so close to the Soviet Union? Because, replied
Bonney, the weather research program is world-wide.

The U-2 did carry Air Force cameras, Bonney said in
reply to another question, but "they are not reconnaissance
cameras. They are cameras to take cloud cover pictures."
The U-2 program, he added, had never been classified
secret.

"We are still searching for the airplane in the Lake
Van area," he said. "It may be a waste of effort. If the
Russians would care to identify the plane as the U-2, a
civilian plane carrying no armament and only research
equipment, then we could stop looking."

In Paris, Mimi Piovene gasped when she picked up a

French newspaper and saw the airplane pictured on page
one under black headlines reporting Khrushchev's speech.
To her, at least, it looked like the plane she had seen at
Sverdlovsk.[2]

On Capitol Hill, there was indignation over the cold-
blooded shooting down by the Soviet Union of an unarmed civilian weather plane as its pilot battled for life
against a faulty oxygen system. Senator Styles Bridges (Republican, N.H.), thought Eisenhower should refuse to go
to the summit conference until he had a proper explanation of the Soviet action.

Senator E. L. Bartlett (Democrat, Alaska) said the
United States should go to the summit in spite of Khrushchev's "provocative remarks." Senator Mike Mansfield
(Democrat, Montana) said it was a fine thing when "the
Russians shoot first and complain later." But he wondered
why NASA was conducting scientific flights where they
might embarrass the President.

At 4:00 P.M., Hagerty held his regular afternoon brief-
ing. He would make no comment on Khrushchev's speech.
Had the inquiry ordered by the President been completed?
"The inquiry as to what the facts show has been com-
pleted." Asked whether the President was aware of the
NASA research flights, Hagerty would not comment.

He announced the President's schedule for the next
day. After a few morning appointments, Eisenhower, at
12:05 P.M., would go to the Armory to look at the AFL-CIO

---

[2] The United States government was so uncertain about what had happened to Powers on May 1 that Ambassador Thompson conducted a personal inquiry into Mrs. Piovene's story that she had seen a U-2 intact at
Sverdlovsk airport. Mrs. Piovene insisted the plane she saw was white;
the U-2 was black. In the end, the C.I.A. discounted the report, but nothing was being ruled out completely.

trade exhibit. At 12:30 P.M., the President would take off
for Gettysburg for the weekend.

At 5:55 P.M., Washington time, the Associated Press
carried this bulletin:

BURBANK, CALIFORNIA, MAY 5.—THE PILOT OF A
U-2 BELIEVED SHOT DOWN OVER RUSSIA LAST SUNDAY
WAS IDENTIFIED BY LOCKHEED AIRCRAFT CORPORATION
TODAY AS FRANCIS G. POWERS, 30.

It was evening in Moscow and Thompson was attending a diplomatic reception at the Sovietskaya Hotel when
a Scandinavian diplomat drifted over to him with an alarming piece of gossip. A moment later another Scandinavian
diplomat told him the same thing.

Thompson did not stop to finish his drink. Unobtru-
sively he left the party, returned to the American Embassy,
and dispatched a warning cable to the State Department.
The warning reached Dillon at 6:00 P.M. Washington time,
just before he went home for the night.

What sent Thompson hurrying away from the reception was a story he had been told by his two Scandinavian
colleagues. A Western diplomat, they said, had asked a
Russian official at the party why the Soviets were so confident they could prove their tale about an American plane
having invaded Soviet air space.

The Russian downed another slug of vodka, looked up
and boasted:

"Because we've got the pilot."

G

7

"No—N-O—No—Deliberate Attempt"

GEORGE M. PULLMAN MADE A fortune on the sleeping cars that bear his name. His former home at 1119 16th Street in Northwest Washington is now the Soviet Embassy. From this building on May 6, a telephone call was placed to the Cuneo Press, in Milwaukee. The Embassy ordered the press run stopped on the forthcoming June issue of *USSR*, the English-language Soviet government publication in America.

A few minor editorial changes were desired, the Embassy explained. On the upper right-hand corner of the cover, over a color photograph of a Russian couple in native costume, the words "Welcome Mr. President" were to be removed, and the words "Income Tax Abolished" substituted.

Inside, a story welcoming Eisenhower to the Soviet Union had explained that while the President's visit would be short, nothing would be hidden, and he would see with his own eyes the progress made since his last visit in 1945. The article, stressing peaceful coexistence, was profusely illustrated with pictures of the President and Khrushchev at Camp David, and scenes from the cities that Eisenhower would visit—Moscow, Leningrad, Kiev, Khabarovsk and Irkutsk.

This story was to be replaced by two others, one on the abolition of the income tax and the other a biographical sketch of Leonid Illyich Brezhnev, who was replacing Voroshilov as President of the Presidium. The aging marshal, the article explained, had been relieved "at his request, because of poor health." [1]

In the ornate committee room of the Senate Foreign Relations Committee on Capitol Hill, Chairman J. William Fulbright, Democrat of Arkansas, had just been told a worrisome bit of news by a high official of the State Department: The department had received news from Moscow that the Russians might—just possibly—have the missing pilot.

In Athens, Herter and the rest of his party emplaned for Madrid. After a one-hour layover at Torrejon Air Force base, the Secretary boarded his aircraft again and headed home for Washington.

In Moscow, Ambassador Thompson received a diplomatic note from Washington inquiring about Powers. He

---

[1] A more plausible reason emerged at the 22nd Communist Party Congress in October, 1961, when Khrushchev finally added Voroshilov to the "anti-party group" that he said had engineered the plot to depose him in 1957.

sent it to the Soviet Foreign Office. He did not go in person because Foreign Minister Andrei A. Gromyko and other top officials were attending the morning session of the Supreme Soviet. The note identified Powers as the civilian pilot of "an unarmed weather research plane" missing since May 1, and requested the "full facts" on the fate of the aircraft and its pilot.

At the Supreme Soviet, Marshal Andrei A. Grechko, commander of Soviet ground forces and First Deputy Minister of Defense, had good news for the deputies. Mounting the same rostrum where Khrushchev had spoken the day before, he reported that the Premier had "personally" given the order to shoot down the American air "pirate." It was accomplished, he said, with a "remarkable rocket" which downed the plane "at the very first shot." The deputies roared their approval.

Gromyko followed with a speech warning that flying geese were sometimes mistaken by United States radar for approaching foreign planes. "If an ordinary goose can be taken for a plane," he said, "a plane can surely be taken for a plane, or at any rate, it cannot be mistaken for a goose."

The claim that the American pilot was unconscious was "absurd." What about the pilots of other American planes that had violated Soviet air space? "Were they unconscious? Are they suggesting that the crews of American planes sent to intrude into the territory of the U.S.S.R. lose consciousness the minute they cross the Soviet border? This is really a new problem for medicine!"

As the team of Grechko and Gromyko regaled the Supreme Soviet, the Soviet trade-union newspaper *Trud* published a photograph of a tangled heap of wreckage which it identified as the remains of the American aircraft. A radio photo of the alleged wreckage was flashed around the world from Moscow. It showed men and children examining the mess. *Pravda* carried a story saying villagers had helped locate "fragments of the American plane" after it was downed.

At Burbank, California, Lockheed officials declined to comment further on the weather plane. "Information about it is highly classified," a Lockheed spokesman announced. "Any releases must come from NASA, which runs the U-2 program." The Lockheed public relations department did not explain why information about a weather plane was highly classified.

At 10:30 A.M., Hagerty held his regular morning briefing with newsmen, announced a few routine nominations and appointments, and handed out a Presidential Mother's Day proclamation. He said the President had been informed of Grechko's speech. He knew of no change in the President's plans to go to the summit and to the Soviet Union. The President and Mrs. Eisenhower had sent a small gift to Princess Margaret, whose marriage to Anthony Armstrong-Jones was now five and a half hours old.

Eisenhower was in a light-hearted mood as he moved about the AFL-CIO trade exhibit at the Armory at noon, with Union President George Meany as his guide. He stopped at a booth and asked Miss Patricia Hiele of Culver City, California, who was shoeless, whether her feet hurt. "They're killing me," she replied, and Eisenhower laughed heartily.

He inspected a model train display erected by the Railway Clerks, a $10,000 all-electric kitchen of the electrical workers. "My goodness," the President said, "they've even got a TV." He also looked at a fallout shelter built by the bricklayers' union. It was being given away as a prize.

At the barbers' union booth, the bald-headed President bumped into Steve Martini, who came to the White House regularly to give him haircuts. "Of course," he said ruefully, "I don't need one very much. I just tell him: 'Clip my neck, please.'"

An exhibit of stoves set the President to reminiscing. "In World War I a man named Harlin came to my tent and offered me a job with the Globe Stove Company of Kokomo, Indiana."

At the bartenders' booth, Eisenhower remarked admiringly: "I see you've got a helluva nice bar."

When he came to the shoe-workers' exhibit, the President was given a pair of union-made white golf shoes and a pair of hunting boots.

At the glass-blowing exhibit, Val Hamer of Baltimore blew a large glass bubble for the beaming President. "Good show," Eisenhower said.

Passing the hull of a Fiberglas boat, the President turned casually to Meany and said, "By the way, I'm taking over to Khrushchev in Moscow, if I go, a boat that has no propeller."

Charles Roberts of *Newsweek*, Robert Pierpoint of C.B.S. and Merriman Smith of UPI were only a few feet away and caught the "if I go."

The newsmen headed speedily for the nearest telephones.

Thompson's warning cable had not filtered down through the State Department ranks. At 12:35 P.M., White,

briefing newsmen, was asked if there had been any change
in orders to United States planes operating near the Soviet
border. He replied: "There is no change to be made. This
gentleman informed us that he was having difficulty with
his oxygen equipment. Now, our assumption is that the
man blacked out. There was absolutely no—N-O—no—deliberate attempt to violate Soviet air space. There never
has been."

Asked about Gromyko's ridicule of the oxygen story,
White replied, "I have no comment, no, except to say
that this is the information which we have, and it is
ridiculous to say that we are trying to kid the world about
this."

Because of the plane's disappearance, NASA announced, it was grounding all U-2's for fifteen days to
permit the checking of equipment, particularly oxygen
systems. A U-2 made a flight out of Edwards Air Force
Base, California, during the day, but a NASA spokesman
blandly announced that the plane's oxygen system had
been checked beforehand. Also at Edwards, the U-2 was
rolled out for public inspection for the first time. It was
shown to a group of visiting aviation writers. They were
allowed to see and photograph the strange black weather
plane. But the cockpit was sealed shut.

Outside the Armory, Eisenhower made a little speech
boosting foreign aid. "As we help our brother," he said,
"we make this a more peaceful, a more prosperous and a
better world in which to live."

At 1:28 P.M., the President climbed into his Marine
helicopter and took off from a field east of the Armory
for Gettysburg. By 3:10 P.M., he was at the Gettysburg
Country Club with George Allen. At the first tee, the

President sent his ball whistling more than two hundred yards down the fairway. A spectator in the gallery drew a laugh when he remarked: "There's not a Democrat in the world who can hit a ball like that."

Hagerty was being pressed by newsmen at his 4:00 P.M. briefing at the White House. Did Eisenhower's "if I go" mean he was thinking about calling off his trip to Russia?

"I have no comment," he replied.

In Moscow, Khrushchev told a visiting parliamentary delegation from Ghana that he would reply tomorrow in the Supreme Soviet to the United States' statement about the plane.

As Khrushchev retired for the night, Barbara Powers, following Shelton's instructions, was flying home from Turkey.

Herter landed in Washington shortly before 5:00 P.M., ending his ten-day trip to Teheran, Istanbul and Athens. He arrived three hours after Eisenhower had left. The President and the Secretary of State would not meet for two more days.

As the Secretary of State stepped into his waiting limousine, Eisenhower and Allen were just coming off the golf course at Gettysburg, chuckling over their good luck. They had played a brisk eighteen holes in two hours.

Both had birdied the par-four eighteenth hole.

▶8

"The President Wants This"

THE SPRING WEATHER WAS particularly pleasant in Moscow on May 7, and the sun streamed through the windows of the Great Hall as Khrushchev strode in at 1:00 P.M., carrying a thick black briefcase. The delegates to the Supreme Soviet applauded as the stocky Premier made his way to the rostrum.

"Comrades," he began, "I must let you in on a secret. When I made my report, I deliberately refrained from mentioning that the pilot was alive and healthy, and that we had the remnants of the plane." The delegates broke into applause. Khrushchev looked around, grinning broadly. He waved his right hand. "We did this deliberately, because had we given out the whole story, the Americans would have thought up another version."

The oxygen-trouble stories, he said, were released because "their authors assumed that if the plane had been shot down, the pilot was probably dead. In that case, there would be nobody to question about what really happened and no way to ascertain the nature of the plane or the type of instruments it carried.

". . . The pilot is safe and sound. He is now in Moscow . . . The pilot's name is Francis G. Powers. He is thirty years old. According to his testimony, he is a First Lieutenant of the U. S. Air Force in which he served up to 1956, when he joined the Central Intelligence Agency.

". . . This was a regular military reconnaissance plane . . . for collecting espionage information . . . Its assignment was to cross the entire territory of the U.S.S.R. from the Pamirs to the Kola Peninsula and photograph military and industrial objectives on Soviet soil."

This time, Ambassador Thompson had taken the precaution of staying away from the Great Hall. He was watching on television, however, at the American Embassy. A second secretary of the Embassy, Lewis W. Bowden, was sitting in a box.

From his black briefcase, Khrushchev pulled out two-foot-square enlarged photographs which he said had been developed from the U-2's spy film.

He brandished them in the general direction of Bowden and cried, "This is a photograph of an airfield. The two white lines are rows of Soviet fighter planes . . . Here are some photographs of petrol depots. It has to be said that the camera used is not a bad one, the photographs are very clear. (Animation.) But it has also to be said that our cameras produce better, sharper pictures, so that in this respect we acquired very little. (Laughter.)"

Khrushchev held up the pictures, shouting repeatedly

in a high-pitched voice: "Here they are! Here they are."
The deputies laughed and cheered. Khrushchev excitedly
handed the pictures to an official, who passed them out
to the Presidium members and other officials behind the
rostrum.

"So that's the kind of air samples this American plane
was taking," Khrushchev said mockingly.

Khrushchev declared that under questioning, "Powers
named some of the officers with whom he served at the
American military base in Turkey. According to him, the
commander of the U.S. 10-10 unit is Colonel William Shelton . . ."

Powers told his interrogators, Khrushchev said, that
his mission was to fly from Peshawar to Bodo, switching
equipment on and off.

He quoted Powers as telling his captors: "I believe
my flight over Soviet territory was meant for collecting
information on Soviet guided missiles and radar stations."

Khrushchev added that Powers had bailed out instead of using his ejection seat. Why, he asked?

"It might be that the plane carried an explosive
charge, to destroy it as soon as the flier catapulted. The
pilot knew that and probably feared he would be killed
in the explosion. Smart man! (Animation.)

"The pilot was told he must not be caught by Soviet
authorities alive. Accordingly, he was given a poison
needle—one jab and death would be instantaneous. What
barbarism! This is the instrument, the latest achievement
in the American technique of killing their own people."

Khrushchev held aloft a photograph of the poison
needle.

"Shame, shame," shouted the deputies.

"But every living thing wants to live, and when the

plane was hit, the pilot bailed out. Nor did he follow the advice of those who sent him on this bandit mission against the Soviet Union."

The Premier shouted that Powers had been given a noiseless pistol. "If the gun was meant for protection against wild animals . . . then why the silencer?" he asked. Rather, said Khrushchev, it was meant "to blow people's brains out! The men who supplied him with the silence gun pray in church and call us godless atheists!

"He had been sent out, we are told, to explore the atmosphere. Yet, he was given 7,500 rubles in Soviet currency . . . Surely he had not made the flight to exchange old rubles for new ones? (Laughter. Stormy applause.)

"He was also given a sum in gold French francs . . . They are enclosed in cellophane—neat American packaging . . . He also had West German, Italian and other currency. Besides his own watch, he was given two gold watches and seven ladies' gold rings. What possible use could he make of all this in the upper strata of the atmosphere? Perhaps he was to have flown still higher, to Mars, and meant to seduce the Martian ladies? (Laughter. Applause.)

"The whole world," Khrushchev added triumphantly, "knows that Allen Dulles is no great authority on meteorology.

". . . I am prepared to grant that the President had no knowledge of a plane being dispatched to the Soviet Union and failing to return. But that should alert us still more . . . when the militarists begin to run the show . . . the result can well be disastrous."

Powers, Khrushchev indicated, had been shot down over Sverdlovsk. He would probably be tried as a spy, Khrushchev said.

He did not bother to add what everyone in the Great Hall knew—a convicted spy might be sentenced to death by shooting.

In Pound, Oliver Powers was out gathering fuel just before dawn when his telephone began ringing insistently. He went inside and answered it. A newspaperman was calling from New York City, asking whether Oliver had heard the latest news.

Oliver said he hadn't, that he'd been asleep all night.

The reporter told him his son had been shot down, brought to Moscow, and was alive and well.

Dumfounded, Oliver managed to reply that he was glad to know his son was still living, no matter where he was.

Ida Powers had overheard her husband on the telephone.

"Thank God he's alive," she told her husband. Then she began to cry. By that time the girls had come in, and the family laughed and cried together.

The harsh jangle of the telephone jarred Lincoln White awake shortly after 6:00 A.M. in the bedroom of his home at 9303 Jessup Lane in Bethesda, a pleasant suburb of Washington. It was a reporter calling to say Khrushchev had announced Powers was alive, in Soviet hands, and had talked.

The phone kept on ringing after that, but White just left it on the cradle. He ate a hasty breakfast and went downtown. At 7:30 A.M., he arrived at his office. He got out a slide rule and maps.

White knew the range of the U-2, as provided by NASA, and it did not take him long to figure out that the

U-2 could never have reached Norway. It would have run out of fuel somewhere in northern Russia. White smiled. He had decided that Khrushchev was wrong.

The President was up bright and early this Saturday. He drove from his farm at the edge of the Civil War battlefield at 8:45 A.M., arriving at the Gettysburg Country Club thirteen minutes later. He teed off at 9:04 A.M., with Arthur Nevins, his farm manager, and George Allen as partners.

In a second-floor, pine-paneled lounge of the Gettysburg Hotel, beneath portraits of Robert E. Lee, Abraham Lincoln and General George Gordon Meade, Hagerty met with newsmen at 9:36 A.M. They had been told he would have a major statement, and although Hagerty had plainly said it would not relate to the U-2, the newsmen suspected it would.

To their surprise, Hagerty announced that the United States, under Project Vela, would resume underground nuclear explosions, to improve its ability to detect and identify such blasts. Out of the confusing discussion that ensued, some newsmen gained the impression that the tests might involve nuclear weapons. "These tests are not weapons tests as such," Hagerty said at one point.

The announcement of renewed United States atomic testing came a few hours after Khrushchev's speech. It was inevitable that the two became linked in many minds as a bellicose United States answer to the spy plane charges.

Hagerty was asked whether the President had been informed of the Khrushchev charges, and if so, how he had reacted. "I told the President about it," Hagerty said (he had informed Eisenhower of the speech before the President left for the golf course). "I have no comment. Any comment that will be made on Mr. Khrushchev's speech will come from the Department of State."

The top intelligence officials of the United States gathered at C.I.A.'s E Street headquarters in Foggy Bottom shortly after 10:00 A.M. to grapple with the crisis now fully upon them.

The Russians apparently had both the U-2 and its elaborate espionage equipment, and, most important of all, its pilot. Khrushchev had struck his fish and he was reeling it in. The meeting must decide what to do now.

Representing the C.I.A. were Dulles, Bissell, and General Charles Pearre Cabell, a pink-faced Texan who had formerly headed Air Force Intelligence. Cumming, Bohlen and Merchant spoke for the State Department. Goodpaster represented the President.

The majority of the men at C.I.A. this Saturday morning were imbued with the ancient, traditional viewpoint toward spying; it was logical that their discussion should reflect it.

The prevailing view, therefore, was that the United States, despite Khrushchev's evidence, including a live pilot, should continue to deny all, much like a husband who is caught in bed with another woman but indignantly claims he is only waiting for the bus to Englewood.

Dulles flatly offered to resign. He argued that this might relieve the pressure on the President, since one can always take the position that the intelligence apparatus has exceeded its authority.

This proposal was debated in front of Dulles, but rejected. Bohlen and Cumming strongly urged continuing the cover story. At one point consideration was given to

picking a low-level scapegoat. The flight would be blamed
on an overeager subordinate in the field. He would be
fired, and his reputation ruined. Months later, he would
quietly be rehabilitated and given another job. Shelton
was not named, but the men at the C.I.A. meeting had in
mind someone on this level of the U-2 operation.

After hours of discussion, a statement was drawn up.
In essence, it continued the cover story, admitting noth-
ing and denying everything. It was after 2:00 P.M. when
Bohlen and Cumming left the meeting together.

In Gettysburg, the President had completed eighteen
holes by 11:28 A.M. He was back on his farm at 11:40 and
remained there for the rest of the day.

White was being deluged with calls from newsmen
asking for State Department reaction to the Khrushchev
speech. He was, for some reason, finding it extremely difficult to locate anybody in a position to give him any
guidance.

In addition to these troubles, he was trying to
straighten out the widespread impression that Hagerty's
announcement on nuclear testing was the United States'
answer to Khrushchev. Word went out from the State Department that there was no connection between the two.
Furthermore, it was made clear, Project Vela would in no
way relate to the development of nuclear weapons.

White attempted all morning to reach Herter and
Dillon, but was told they were briefing Latin American
ambassadors on the results of the NATO meeting. He
learned, finally, that Bohlen and Cumming were meeting
across the street at C.I.A.

Unable to contact any of the principal officers of the department, White suspected for the first time that something was amiss.

"Oh, Jesus," he said softly.

In Minneapolis, Harold E. Stassen decided to make a statement to the press. He telephoned the AP in Washington and charged that the U-2 had been sent deliberately by "some of our military officers" to blow up the summit meeting scheduled to start May 16.

Stassen, embittered former disarmament adviser to Eisenhower, said these officers "know full well the reaction and counteraction which such flights cause and the adverse effects on the chances for progress in the negotiation at the summit." He added:

"I doubt that President Eisenhower knew about or approved this flight. If he did not, he should remove the officers involved from their command, no matter how high up they may be."

At Idlewild International Airport in New York, Barbara Powers, weary after her flight across the ocean, was met by William O. Miller, a Lockheed public relations man from Washington. He had been impressed into service by the C.I.A. to shepherd Barbara back to Milledgeville. The two flew to Atlanta, rented a car, and began driving south to Milledgeville.

On the road south, Barbara suddenly remembered it was Mother's Day. She wanted to buy a present. At Griffin, Georgia, they stopped off at a restaurant. Afterwards, Miller suggested she go to a drugstore across the street to buy the present. Barbara purchased a compact

H

for her mother and happened to glance at a newspaper.
Her picture was on the front page alongside that of Gary.
The headline said he had been shot down and was a
prisoner of the Russians.

She was barely able to walk back across the street
to the car.

Cumming and Bohlen entered the State Department
by the north basement entrance on E Street. They went to
Herter's office on the fifth floor. There a meeting was
already in progress. Seated in chairs and on sofas were
Herter, Dillon, Foy D. Kohler,[1] the Assistant Secretary for
European Affairs, and Richard H. Davis, his deputy. Mer-
chant and Goodpaster, who had been across the street at
C.I.A., also joined the meeting. Dulles remained at C.I.A.

Dillon, who had been at the helm of the department
until Friday night, was bringing Herter, Kohler, and the
other officials who had been in Turkey up to date on what
had happened.

For the most part the officials who had been away
during the week had a different perspective from the
intelligence people who had remained in Washington.
Herter and Kohler both felt that the espionage flight was
no longer deniable. In Kohler's view, the cover story had
been destroyed and they were now engaged in a salvage
operation. Herter felt the cover story had been inadequate
from the start and that White, under pressure from reporters, had gone too far the previous day in denying
United States overflights.

Herter read the draft brought from the C.I.A. by

---

[1] Kohler was one of the small group in the department who knew about
the spy program; he had officially been let in on the secret of the U-2
in 1958.

Cumming. He did not concur. Since Khrushchev had revealed that the plane was down deep inside Russia, and that Powers was talking, he felt that there would have to be an admission of espionage.

Kohler had drawn up a draft statement admitting the spy flight and indicating it had been sent by the President.

The Secretary of State argued that it was not necessary to involve the President, however. The President, Herter felt, knew less about the details of the program than he did. It might be possible to protect the President.

Herter was the man in the middle; he attempted to reconcile the two drafts. Dillon, who had been siding with Cumming and Bohlen, now swung over to Herter's position; he argued that the truth about the flight could no longer be denied.

Herter ordered a new statement drawn up, confessing the spy flight, but seeking to justify it on the grounds that Soviet secrecy left no other choice.

Cumming called Dulles across the street to let him know how the tide was flowing. The C.I.A. director was very disturbed by Cumming's report.

In the meantime, Herter called Eisenhower.

A Filipino houseboy answered the phone in the President's study at Gettysburg, and then stepped out onto the porch where the President and Hagerty were sitting.

"Mr. President," he said, "the Secretary of State is calling."

Eisenhower and Hagerty moved inside. Herter informed Eisenhower that he had drafted a statement admitting espionage but not implicating the President in the flight.

Eisenhower objected. He argued that he wanted to

take full responsibility. He felt it his "duty." He did not
wish to pass off responsibility on a subordinate. It would
not be honorable. Hagerty shared the President's view.

Herter countered that the President did not have to
assume responsibility because he was, in fact, not intimately connected with the U-2 program. Eisenhower did
not seem upset at Khrushchev's speech, but conceded
that the Soviet leader had the United States over a barrel.

Before the telephone call had ended, Herter had succeeded in convincing Eisenhower not to take responsibility. The President reluctantly went along with the
Secretary of State.

From time to time during the U-2 program, thought
had been given to letting Lincoln White in on the secret.
The suggestion was always rejected.

Two or three times during the afternoon, White burst
in on the meeting in Herter's office, panting: "I've got to
have a statement." Each time this occurred, all would
clam up until White had left. Then the discussions would
continue. Now, as the afternoon came to a close, White
was about to have his wish granted.

When the new draft was completed, Goodpaster took
it and went to a phone at the other end of the room. When
he came back the statement had a new sentence added
to it:

"As a result of the inquiry ordered by the President,
it has been established that insofar as the authorities in
Washington are concerned, there was no authorization for
any such flight as described by Mr. Khrushchev."

"The President wants this," Goodpaster told the meeting.

He added that Eisenhower had personally dictated the sentence to him.

That settled it. The meeting's work was over.

The new draft, however, had to be retyped so that no one, including White, would ever know the earlier version. Shortly after six o'clock White was summoned to the office and handed a piece of paper.

White paled, shook his head helplessly, and sat down. "W-wait a minute," he said. "I've got to read this."

When he had finished he turned to Bohlen and asked him to come downstairs with him to help answer questions from the press.

"You'd better just stick to what's on that paper," Bohlen replied.

White went down to face the reporters, alone.

At 6:00 P.M., the crestfallen White appeared before the newsmen. He had told them twenty-nine hours earlier that "there was absolutely no—N-O—no—deliberate attempt to violate Soviet air space." Now he began reading:

"The Department has received the text of Mr. Khrushchev's further remarks about the unarmed plane which is reported to have been shot down in the Soviet Union. As previously announced, it was known that a U-2 plane was missing. As a result of the inquiry ordered by the President, it has been established that insofar as the authorities in Washington are concerned, there was no authorization for any such flight as described by Mr. Khrushchev.

"Nevertheless, it appears that in endeavoring to obtain information now concealed behind the Iron Curtain, a flight over Soviet territory was probably undertaken by an unarmed civilian U-2 plane.

"It is certainly no secret that given the state of the

world today, intelligence collection activities are practiced by all countries, and postwar history certainly reveals that the Soviet Union has not been lagging behind in this field. The necessity for such activities as measures for legitimate national defense is enhanced by the excessive secrecy practiced by the Soviet Union in contrast to the Free World.

"One of the things creating tension in the world today is apprehension over surprise attack with weapons of mass destruction. To reduce mutual suspicion and to give a measure of protection against surprise attack, the United States in 1955 offered its 'Open Skies' proposal—a proposal which was rejected out of hand by the Soviet Union. It is in relation to the danger of surprise attack that planes of the type of unarmed civilian U-2 aircraft have made flights along the frontiers of the Free World for the past four years."

Reporters pressed White on what the words "probably" undertaken meant. Who had sent the plane if it was not authorized in Washington? White was sorry; he could not elaborate.

For the first time in its 184-year history, the government of the United States had conceded publicly that it had deliberately lied, that it had committed espionage, and violated the territory of another country.

The statement was purposely fuzzy and much of it was still untrue: the assertion that nobody in Washington had authorized the flight, the vagueness about the flight having been "probably" undertaken, the identification of the combined C.I.A.-Air Force plane as "civilian," and the cloudy reference to flights "along the frontiers."

The bulletin spread rapidly among the incredulous

members of the National Press Club, at 14th and F streets. One of them was Valentin M. Ivanov,[2] First Secretary of the Soviet Embassy, a short, pudgy man with thick glasses. A habitué of the club, he played in the chess tournaments and picked up what intelligence he could.

At 6:18 P.M., Ivanov dashed out of the Press Club, unable to contain himself.

He was shouting one word, over and over again: "Admitted! Admitted! Admitted!"

[2] The United States expelled Ivanov August 13, 1960, in retaliation for the ouster of American diplomats and tourists during a spy scare whipped up in Moscow in advance of the Powers trial. Ivanov was accused of paying $500 to a young member of the self-styled "American Nazi Party" to induce him to obtain a job with the United States government.

9

To Paris, in the Spring

THE PRESIDENT'S DOMESTIC critics and Nikita Sergeyevich Khrushchev had one thing in common: Both sought to picture Eisenhower as a President who was not master in his own house.

Eisenhower's Democratic foes relished charging that the President spent too much time away from the job, golfing with his big-business cronies and quail shooting in Georgia. The Democrats maintained that the President was insulated from reality and the problems of his office by a rigid staff system he had himself imposed. Particularly while Sherman Adams was running the White House staff, they claimed, the President received only predigested, carefully strained position papers devoid of controversy and condensed for quick, easy perusal.

On his part, Khrushchev pictured Eisenhower as a nice, sincere fellow but a captive of the "aggressive imperialist forces" and "Pentagon militarists" and their "monopoly associates," who Khrushchev said really ran the country.

On Saturday, May 7, with a Presidential election coming in the fall, Eisenhower had reinforced both the image dearly cherished by the domestic political opposition and that held by Khrushchev. While an unprecedented decision was being made, in which the United States admitted it had lied, spied, and violated Soviet air space, the President was golfing and relaxing at Gettysburg.

He had ended up by taking Herter's advice to avoid personal responsibility for the U-2 mission. The statement made it clear that, precisely as Khrushchev had intimated, the flight had not been authorized by the President.

In both his speeches to the Supreme Soviet, Khrushchev had been careful not to blame the spy flight on the President. On the surface it appeared that Khrushchev was encouraging Eisenhower to disavow the U-2, and perhaps fire Dulles.

Both times, however, Khrushchev had warned that if Eisenhower did not send the plane, and it was the work of "Pentagon militarists," then the world was indeed in difficulty. "How can people feel safe when war or peace . . . depends on men capable of playing with fire?" Khrushchev had asked.

The wily Soviet Premier had posed for the President a horned dilemma. If Eisenhower had sent the plane, then the President was responsible not only for the flight but for the lies thereafter. If he did not, then Khrushchev was right, Eisenhower was indeed a captive of the C.I.A., which was flying espionage missions behind his back.

It was a bit like the Salem witch test. If a suspect swam when thrown into the water, she was considered a witch and promptly burned at the stake. If she sank, she was considered innocent.

Hagerty, who was at the President's side this weekend at Gettysburg, was particularly sensitive to the charge that Eisenhower was not on the job. He had worked hard, and on the whole successfully, to counter the Democratic image of a lazy President.

The more Eisenhower thought about the situation, the more strongly he felt about it. Overnight, he reversed his decision. He would personally and publicly assume responsibility for an act of espionage.

Later, stories went the rounds in Washington that Hagerty was solely responsible for the President's decision. The press secretary disagreed. Hagerty had believed the President should have taken the responsibility, but Herter's arguments had prevail~d at least on Saturday afternoon.

Normally the President returned from Gettysburg on Monday morning. This time he decided to go back to the White House on Sunday afternoon. He would meet there with Herter.

During the morning the President attended services at Gettysburg Presbyterian Church. On his left lapel he wore a huge white carnation for Mother's Day. He stopped for a brief chat on the way out of church with the Reverend Robert A. MacAskill.

In the afternoon, he drove in a downpour back to the White House.

Hagerty was in the car with the President.

In Karachi and Ankara the Soviet pressure on the

smaller nations involved in the U-2 flight was beginning to be felt. Pakistani Foreign Secretary Mohammed Ikramullah said in London that his country had no information that the U-2 had stopped off in Peshawar. But an inquiry had been ordered, he said, and if the charge was true, a protest would be filed with the United States.

In Ankara the teetering Turkish government said it had not given permission for any American plane to fly over the Soviet Union from Turkey and none had. "Soviet authorities have not contradicted this," the Turks declared.[1]

Shortly before 6:00 P.M. Sunday, the President met in his upstairs study at the White House with Herter, Hagerty, and Goodpaster. Because of Herter's travels and Eisenhower's trip to Gettysburg, it was the first time the President and the Secretary of State had met since the U-2 was reported overdue the previous Sunday.

Eisenhower informed Herter that he had changed his mind about the Saturday statement. He told him to announce the flight had been sent by Presidential authority. He ordered a new statement drafted. It was the first time in American history that a President had taken personal, public responsibility for conducting espionage.

The men in the White House study went to work.

The President came down to breakfast Monday morning, May 9, with a splotch of iodine behind his left ear. He explained to fourteen Republican Congressmen who breakfasted with him that he had been assailed by a mos-

---

1 In the aftermath of the U-2 incident, diplomatic notes crisscrossed in a maze. Russia protested to Norway, Pakistan, and Turkey. Norway, Pakistan, and Afghanistan protested to the United States. And, of course, Washington and Moscow were protesting to each other.

quito. The insect, he told Representative Bob Wilson of California, had bitten him smack on a scar from a West Point football injury. The Congressmen laughed.

Over coffee and rolls, the President steered the conversation into politics and the November elections. He would do some campaigning, he said. Only once did the subject on everyone's mind come up. The President was asked, gingerly, about the U-2. He replied that a carefully prepared statement on the matter had been issued Saturday night. He preferred to stand on that.

At 9:30 A.M., Anne Wheaton, associate White House press secretary, denied a story in that morning's *New York Times* by James Reston. The article said the President had ordered a halt to all flights "over or near" Communist frontiers. An hour later, Hagerty, acting with Eisenhower's approval, issued a similar denial. These protestations led to the first stirrings of what became a widespread impression that the U-2 flights might continue.

Hagerty's news conference was brisk:

Q. Who did authorize the flight?

A. I have no comment.

Q. Why is such information withheld?

A. I have no comment.

Q. Was the President aware of the U-2 flights?

A. I have no comment.

Q. Who did the pilot work for?

A. I have no comment.

At eleven o'clock a meeting was held in Herter's office to complete the draft of the new statement. Present, in addition to the Secretary of State, were Dillon, Kohler, Bohlen, Gates and James H. Douglas, Jr., Deputy Secretary of Defense.

Bohlen stubbornly opposed the assumption of Presidential responsibility for the spy flight, but he was quickly overruled. The decision had already been made by Eisenhower, and this was merely a drafting session to work out the language.

The statement which came out of this meeting largely followed the lines of Kohler's original draft on Saturday, which had been discarded.

The new statement admitted that aerial spying, including overflights, had been conducted for years under Presidential directives. It left the strong implication they might continue. It blamed the Soviet Union for making such flights necessary.

When their work was completed, Herter attempted to call the President and read the statement to him. Eisenhower had left his office by this time, however, and was in the Executive Mansion eating lunch. Herter sent out for a sandwich. Shortly afterwards, he was able to reach the President and read the text of the new statement to him.

The President approved. Herter's secretary began typing it up.

While the statement was being hammered out behind closed doors in Herter's office, Oliver Powers announced in Pound that he had appealed to Khrushchev "as one old coal miner to another" to "be fair to my boy" and send him home. In Moscow, Malinovsky told 15,000 cheering Russians at a V-E Day ceremony at the Sports Palace that air bases provided by United States "accomplices" could easily be "wiped out." Norwegian Ambassador to Washington Paul Koht asked for and received an appointment with Herter to "inquire" about the Soviet charge that the U-2 was headed for Bodo. And in Atlanta, Senator Richard B. Russell, chairman of the Senate Armed Services Committee, said that the United States was "almost incredibly stupid" to overfly Russia just before the summit. "It was just like a boy getting caught with his hand in the cookie jar," Russell drawled.

Russell was not the only one who was angry. Congress demanded an explanation of the confusing events of the past few days. Dulles and Herter were "invited" to appear before a select group of eighteen Congressional leaders from both houses. Members had to knock on a locked door, and, for them to be let in, their names had to appear on a list.

Reporters outside could glimpse a gray Navy blanket that had been hung over the inside of the entrance to screen the interior and muffle voices. Senator Frank J. Lausche, Democrat of Ohio, was politely shown out when it developed his name was not on the list.

Herter and Dulles arrived together at 2:02 P.M. When asked if he would have any statement after the meeting, the C.I.A. director smiled and replied, "About the usual." Reporters laughed, since Dulles never had a reputation as a chatterbox.

There was no transcript made of the cloak-and-dagger session, but participants reported later that Dulles showed pictures brought back by the U-2's remarkable camera and declared he had no information that the plane was hit by a rocket. He also expressed full confidence in Powers and cited the pilot's excellent four-year record, perhaps partly to stem rumblings that Powers might be a double agent. He asserted that the Soviet Union had not made flights over the United States, except in the area of Alaska.

Herter gave the lawmakers an advance rundown on the statement drafted in his office.

When the ninety-minute briefing ended, House Speaker Sam Rayburn, surrounded by reporters, waved his hands high over his head to indicate he would have nothing at all to say. Herter and Dulles, moving slowly because the Secretary of State used crutches, were trailed from the Capitol by the newsmen. The reporters got no comment, but one of them overheard Dulles remark to Herter: "That was a rough one."

At 3:55 P.M., eighteen minutes after Dulles and Herter had stepped out of the frying pan on Capitol Hill, Lincoln White walked into the press briefing room at the State Department and handed out what was the fourth United States statement on the spy plane in five days. It was issued under Herter's name.

Ever since Stalin began the cold war, it said, the world had lived in a state of "apprehension with respect to Soviet intentions." Within their tightly closed society, the Russians might be building up for a nuclear sneak attack.

Moscow, it added, had rejected United States proposals for "Open Skies" and disarmament. It was "unacceptable" that the Soviet Union be allowed to make "secret preparations" for nuclear war.

"The government of the United States would be derelict to its responsibility not only to the American people, but to free peoples everywhere if it did not, in the absence of Soviet cooperation, take such measures as are possible unilaterally to lessen and to overcome this danger of surprise attack. In fact the United States has not and does not shirk this responsibility.

"In accordance with the National Security Act of 1947, the President has put into effect since the beginning of his Administration directives to gather by every possible means the information required to protect the United States and the Free World against surprise attack and to enable them to make effective preparations for their defense. Under these directives programs have been developed and put into operation which have included extensive aerial surveillance by unarmed civilian aircraft, normally of a peripheral character but on occasion by penetration. Specific missions of these unarmed civilian aircraft have not been subject to Presidential authorization."

The flights, the statement said, were no secret to the Russian leaders. "Far from being damaging to the forthcoming meeting in Paris," it added, "this incident should serve to underline the importance to the world of . . . safeguards against surprise attack and aggression."

White had finished reading. The questions began, but White, as a spokesman and not a policy-maker, could add little:

Q. Linc, the logical question which arises is, will such aerial surveillance . . . continue?

A. I am sorry, on these questions I just cannot answer . . . I am not going to guesstimate on something that I do not know specifically.

Q. I didn't want to shirk the responsibility of questioning.

A. I don't want to shirk the responsibility of answering, but I do not have any specific information . . .

Q. You realize that a normal interpretation of this would be that we intend to continue.

A. Well, I will leave it to your interpretation.

What the reporters did not know was that the statement drafted in Herter's office several hours earlier was deliberately ambiguous on the question of future U-2 flights. The men who drafted the statement purposely "fuzzed it up," as one of the participants confided later.

One of the oldest gambits in government public relations is to phrase a statement in such a way that the press must, in order to do its job properly, infer a conclusion that is not quite stated.

The officials who drafted the Herter statement knew that the press would have to say the Secretary of State had indicated that the flights might continue. But the Secretary of State could later say, truthfully, that he had never really said so. In the meantime, it would keep the Russians, and the rest of the world, guessing.

There was a reason for this. As the Paris summit approached, Eisenhower's temper began to flare behind the scenes. To his intimates at the White House he said, in effect: We're not going to have any more of these damn flights, but we won't say so.

Eisenhower made it clear to his inner circle of advisers that he considered the flights a "blown" instrument of espionage and that they would have to stop. At the same time, he was not going to let Khrushchev—he pronounced it "Crook-chef"—dictate policy to the United States. There would, therefore, be no more flights, but no announcement either.

As the questioning of White indicated, the majority of newsmen and news media, although not all, took Herter's statement to mean the flights would continue, in defiance of Khrushchev's protests.

Both major wire services, pumping news to the newspapers and radio and television stations in the nation and the world, played the story this way. UPI's first lead said:

THE UNITED STATES ADMITTED CONDUCTING "EX-TENSIVE AERIAL SURVEILLANCE" OVER AND AROUND RUSSIA AND HINTED IT WOULD CONTINUE . . .

I

AP's night lead, by John Scali, said:

THE STATE DEPARTMENT DID NOT DISCOURAGE A
DEDUCTION THAT SUCH FLIGHTS MAY CONTINUE . . .

Scali had put his finger on an important point. If the
White House and the State Department had not desired to
give this impression, Hagerty or White, or both, could
have corrected it within seconds of the time the first bulle-
tins hit the wire. This is often done when officials feel a
story is moving out incorrectly. But it was not done this
time.

That night, in a six-column streamer, the *New York
Times* interpreted the statement the way most papers did:

HERTER INDICATES FLIGHTS WILL GO ON.

In Burbank, Kelly Johnson announced that the Soviet
photo of the alleged U-2 wreckage was a fake. "After
spending the best part of the weekend analyzing the photo
with my top technical people," said Johnson, "I am convinced that the Russians, for some reason, have released
the pictures of some other airplane crash." Johnson thought
the photograph was of a Russian Beagle bomber.

At NASA, Dryden and Bonney [2] had some explaining
to do to newsmen. "I thought I was telling the truth," Bonney explained. Dryden did not go quite so far. He said he
thought planes were being used for a "legitimate purpose"
of learning about wind gusts. But Dryden confessed he had
been aware that the planes were also being used for gathering air samples from Soviet atomic tests.

---

[2] Bonney left the government November 15, 1960, to return to private
industry and forget the U-2.

. . .

At the Czechoslovak Embassy reception in Moscow, the clink of glasses subsided as Khrushchev began to speak. He did not know yet that Eisenhower had assumed responsibility in the new statement just being issued in Washington.

"It is said that it was the work of the military," Khrushchev stormed. "How can the government tolerate this? What kind of a state is this? . . . The statement that the aggressive flight was made without the will and instructions of the State Department does not do any credit to the State Department . . . and what about Allen Dulles? He knew all about this . . . It is Allen Dulles' aviation!"

Khrushchev announced that the day after General Twining left Russia in 1956, a United States plane flew "as far as Kiev . . . at great altitude. All that Twining may be compared to is an animal that does its dirty doings right where it eats. From his behavior we drew the right conclusion—we concentrated on rockets and fighters . . . The rocket finds the target itself!"

It was the first time that Khrushchev had publicly [3] admitted that the overflights had been going on for years, a fact he carefully omitted in his first speech. Now he apparently felt confident enough to reveal this.

After the April 9 flight succeeded, he said, "the American military" wanted to try again. "Well, Khrushchev, they seemed to say, what are you boasting of? We fly over your country and you can do nothing about it. They expected to fly over Soviet territory this time, too, to fly over Sverdlovsk and to show that we could do nothing about it. It was

[3] Khrushchev's remarks about the 1956 Kiev overflight never appeared in the Soviet press, however. Russian citizens were told of no specific overflights other than those on April 9 and May 1, 1960.

an unpleasant situation indeed. And now . . . we have
hit the air pirate with a rocket."

In a joking manner, Khrushchev managed to dispose
of the argument that if and when a U-2 were caught, the
Russians would never dare admit it.

Then he turned his attention to Thompson, standing
nearby.

"I respect the Ambassador of the United States," he
said, "and I am convinced that he had nothing to do with
this incursion . . . I am sure of his moral standards . . .
I suppose he is feeling very bad about it, looking at it as a
very unpleasant thing both for his country, the U.S.A., and
for himself as its representative in the Soviet Union. So,
we've got to take this into consideration."

Thompson, who had been trying to duck Khrushchev,
was embarrassed. The Ambassador had never been told
about the U-2 flights, and was flabbergasted when Khrushchev had disclosed Powers' capture. Such was his relationship with the Soviet leader, that even at the height of the
U-2 crisis, Khrushchev went out of his way to absolve him
of any connection with the flight.

Khrushchev took Pakistani Ambassador Salman Ali
aside and warned that Peshawar had been marked on a
map and pinpointed by Soviet rockets. He gave a similar
warning to Oscar Gundersen, the Norwegian Ambassador.

But he left Thompson alone this night. Weeks later,
at another reception and in another mood, Khrushchev
called Thompson forward and began berating him about
the U-2 flight.

Thompson replied coolly, "You've been flying over
Alaska and elsewhere."

Khrushchev stepped on the United States Ambassador's toe and snapped, "If you do that, you should say excuse me."

The other diplomats were holding their breath, but Thompson refused to be goaded into an argument.

"Come on," he told Khrushchev, "let's have a drink and go on home."

Thompson and Khrushchev had a drink, and went on home.

The final week before the summit meeting was one of rising tension between Washington and Moscow.

On Tuesday, May 10, Gromyko summoned Edward Freers to the Soviet Foreign Ministry. He was chargé d'affaires in the absence of Thompson, who had left for Paris and the summit that morning.

The expressionless Russian handed Freers a note which for the first time officially informed the United States that one of its planes had invaded Soviet air space.

The lengthy note said Powers would be tried as a spy and that Washington had now admitted overflights were a "calculated state policy." It added that Washington was arbitrarily "opening" the skies of other countries because the Soviet Union had rejected the Eisenhower "Open Skies" proposal in 1955. It charged the State Department had declared the United States intended to continue the overflights.

In return, Freers gave Gromyko a two-paragraph note asking that an Embassy official be allowed to interview Powers.

In Washington, the State Department moved to counter the Soviet threat of missile attacks on the smaller nations implicated in the U-2 affair. White emphasized that the United States would defend its allies in the event of an attack. At the White House, it was announced that the President would go through with plans to visit Japan and Korea in June even if he had to cancel his trip to the Soviet Union. "That is firm," Mrs. Wheaton announced.[4]

On Capitol Hill, an uneasy truce prevailed, with Democrats generally closing ranks in support of the Administration because of the oncoming heads-of-government meeting. Senator Lyndon B. Johnson adopted the statesmanlike stance of a Presidential hopeful. But the Texas Democrat's bipartisanship was tempered by a promise of a future Congressional investigation "if blunders have been made."

The President met during the afternoon with his political heir, Vice-President Nixon, the certain Republican Presidential candidate in November. Much less certain was who would be Nixon's Democratic opponent. Even as the two men met at the White House, however, that question was being decided. From the backwoods and coal fields of depressed West Virginia, the voters were going to the polls this day to choose Senator John F. Kennedy of Massachusetts over Hubert H. Humphrey, the ebullient Senator from Minnesota.

On Wednesday in Moscow, five hundred correspondents vied for position outside the Chess Pavilion in the Gorki Central Park of Culture and Rest. They were being let inside in groups of fifty to view an exhibition of the

---

[4] On June 16, while in Manila, Eisenhower was asked to cancel his visit to Japan. Premier Nobusuke Kishi said he could no longer guarantee the President's safety because of left-wing riots against the Japanese–U.S. Security Treaty. The U-2 incident was one of the causes of the demonstrations.

remains of the U-2, Powers' spy equipment, personal effects, and his signed confession of espionage.

Unexpectedly a big Zil limousine drove up, followed by a bodyguard car. Out popped Khrushchev, who bustled inside through an exit door, to be taken on a special preview of the exhibit.

"Experts" armed with pointers and a ready speech about each piece of equipment explained the exhibit to Khrushchev as he moved through the Pavilion, which was about half the size of a basketball court.

One wall was lined with glass cases containing Powers' identification cards, currency, survival kit, and the like. Khrushchev moved past the cases, displaying $225 in twenties, tens, fives, and singles, a stack of West German marks, Turkish notes, forty-eight gold Napoleon francs in two cellophane packages, Italian lire, and two packets containing 7,500 Soviet rubles.

Exhibited as well were a Defense Department Uniformed Services and Privileges Identification card, No. 288,068, which had been pieced together from half a dozen segments, as though someone had tried to tear it into small pieces.

It identified Powers as a civilian employee of the Air Force, assigned to "Department 10" with unlimited PX privileges. It was signed by Captain Ray A. Soelberg, USAF.

There was certainly no effective attempt by C.I.A. to disguise Powers' identity on the May 1 flight. In addition to his official Defense Department card, he flew over Russia carrying a Social Security card, No. 230–30–0321, a Selective Service card, No. 44112727329, issued in Pound, Virginia, a Georgia driver's license, No. 2571132, four seven-cent United States air mail stamps (the kind showing a four-engine jet plane), a receipt for his car from a West German garage; medical certificates; and two cards rating him for instrument flying, issued at Bolling Air Force Base, Washington. He also carried several photographs of Barbara, including one honeymoon pose of the two of them holding hands in a night club.

Powers also had seven wedding bands and four American watches for barter, a pocket cooker of German manufacture, a half-empty pack of Kent cigarettes, two pocket knives, two compasses, a night flare, a saw, a tube of morphine, fishing tackle, a flashlight, the .22 noiseless pistol with 205 Remington standard-velocity cartridges, a hunting knife, and a collapsible rubber boat.

The 1¼-inch curare-tipped poison needle was also on view. The needle was inside a protective casing, a pin with a hole bored in the center. On the point of the needle were deep furrows covered with a thick, sticky brownish mass—curare.

Powers' flight chart, with the route from Peshawar to Bodo marked in different-colored pencils, was displayed nearby.

On the opposite wall were the pilot's green nylon pressure suit, his white helmet and face plate, oxygen tanks, and an orange and white parachute, packed. Here also was the U-2's Pratt & Whitney J-75 engine. Mounted in the center of the room were the wings, which appeared to have been dismantled from the fuselage.

They bore no insignia and were punctured in several places with what some Western military attachés later thought were holes filed by hand. The right wing was shorter and had suffered more damage at the tip than the left wing.

The tail assembly carried no visible markings either. Chunks were missing and the metal was jagged.

Khrushchev stopped to study the ejection seat, which was separately mounted, and badly twisted. He also paused to view the destructor unit, an ominous-looking oblong metal box with two leads for electrical connections, perched atop a round explosive container the size and shape of a layer cake. The manufacturer's printed label read "DESTRUCTOR UNIT," and underneath, "Beckman & Whitley, Inc."

Also on view was a camera, badly battered, but clearly marked "Model 73-B," with a focal length of thirty-six inches. One piece of the fuselage showed seven grapefruit-sized portholes for the camera.

One of the guides switched on a tape recorder for Khrushchev. "Now you will hear the signals of our radar stations recorded by Powers," he said.

"Bleep, Bleep, Bleep," went the tape.

"An exchange of technical knowledge," Khrushchev cracked.

A photocopy of the typed record of Powers' confession was on view, with the pilot's signature in four places.

Beady-eyed Secret Police agents in blue-banded hats stood behind each display.

Khrushchev stopped to read a silk cloth on which was printed an American flag and, in fourteen languages, the message:

"I am an American and do not speak your language. I need food, shelter and assistance. I will not harm you. I bear no malice toward your people. If you will help me, you will be rewarded."

The message appeared not only in English and Russian, but, interestingly, in Hungarian, Lithuanian, Bulgarian, Rumanian, Czech and Polish. Powers' instructions had been to try to land anywhere but in Russia in case of trouble.

As Khrushchev began moving out of the building, he was surrounded by reporters who had gained entrance before his arrival. "May I ask you a question?" one of the correspondents inquired. "You may even ask two questions," replied Khrushchev airily.

Mikhail Kharlamov, Soviet Press Chief, and Sasha Besmertnikh, a Foreign Office spokesman, came running out to where the rest of the correspondents were waiting. They singled out the Americans and said that Khrushchev was about to say something of interest. With that, they hustled the Americans inside. Then the rest of the foreign and Soviet press were cleared in.

The Premier of the Soviet Union spied a wicker chair near the exit and hopped up on it. There, for more than an hour, he held an extraordinary unscheduled press conference.

"Would the plane episode affect Eisenhower's visit to Moscow?" a newsman asked.

"I would not like to be in Mr. Eisenhower's place," replied Khrushchev. But the Soviet people are "very polite, so there will be no excesses."

Then he angrily attacked Herter's May 9 statement as "outrageous." Khrushchev's face became contorted. His teeth were grinding and veteran correspondents had never seen him outwardly so furious.

"Herter's statement," he said, "has made us doubt the correctness of our earlier conclusions that the President . . . did not know about the flights.

"We are not in a state of war with America. These

aggressive actions are impudence, sheer impudence!" [5]

He went on: "We do not live according to the laws of the United States. We have our own laws and this is why we shall make everyone on our territory respect these laws —and the violators will be thrashed!

"If we accept the philosophy which some people in the United States want . . . it is not the burglar that is guilty, but the owner of the house he broke into, because he locked it, thereby compelling the burglar to break in.

"But this is a philosophy of thieves and bandits!"

A reporter asked, "Do you still want President Eisenhower to come to the Soviet Union?"

Khrushchev paused for about forty-five seconds, his brow knotted. Up to this point he had not ruled out Eisenhower's trip.

Now he replied: "What shall I say? Take my place and say it for me . . . You know my attitude toward the President of the United States. I have often spoken about it. But my hopes have been disappointed. I am a man and have human feelings. I am responsible for the direction of the Soviet government . . . So how can I now call on our people to turn out and welcome the dear guest that is coming to us. The people will say: Are you nuts? What kind of a dear guest is he who allows a plane to fly to us to spy? The American militarists . . . have put me . . . in a very difficult position. Frankly speaking, I think the United States President understands this himself.

"Supposing, before my visit to the United States, we had sent such a plane over there and they had shot it down.

5 Khrushchev may have had second thoughts about his strong words, because Moscow censors held up his press conference for twenty-four hours. Some newsmen managed to phone out a few paragraphs before the lines were cut.

One can imagine the kind of welcome I would have got from the Americans. They would have met me according to my just deserts. I think everybody understands that."

Later, newsmen wondered if in the forty-five-second wait, Khrushchev, 1) was making up his mind whether to allow Eisenhower to come·to Russia or, 2) had already decided to bar Eisenhower and was debating whether to indicate this to the reporters.

Khrushchev added another news item: He intended to arrive in Paris on Saturday, two days before the conference started, "in order to get acclimatized a little." He added: "I like Paris, it's a nice city."

Across the street from the White House, in the conference room of the Executive Office Building, 275 perspiring reporters were fighting unsuccessfully to find knee-room amid the closely set rows of metal folding chairs.

Normally, Eisenhower arrived with military precision at 10:30 A.M. This time, he walked in very slowly at 10:27 A.M., accompanied by Hagerty and the matronly Mrs. Wheaton.

"Good morning," the President said to the reporters in a low, serious voice. "Please sit down. I have made some notes from which I want to talk to you about this U-2 incident."

The President reached into his inside jacket pocket for the notes, then donned a pair of spectacles with transparent plastic rims.

"After that," he added, "I shall have nothing to say—for the simple reason I can think of nothing to add that might be useful at this time."

The President declared that espionage "is a distasteful but vital necessity . . . no one wants another Pearl Har-

bor . . . In the Soviet Union there is a fetish of secrecy
and concealment. This is a major cause of international
tension . . ." As Herter had stated, ever since the beginning of his Administration, "I have issued directives to
gather, in every feasible way, the information required to
protect the United States and the free world against surprise attack . . ."

Intelligence operations, he added, are "below the surface activities . . . we must not be distracted by the real
issues of the day by what is an incident or a symptom of
the world situation today."

As to his Moscow trip, Eisenhower, not yet aware of
Khrushchev's wicker-chair press conference, said one could
never tell from one day to the next, but "I expect to go."

The outlook for the summit, he added, had not changed
"decisively at all." The President also told his news conference that he could not see why Khrushchev was making
such a fuss over the U-2.

"And I'll tell you this: The United States and none of
its allies that I know of has engaged in nothing that could
be considered honestly as provocative.

"We are looking to our own security and our defense
and we have no idea of promoting any kind of conflict or
war. This is just, it's absolutely ridiculous and they know
it is."

The Administration came in for subdued criticism by
Adlai E. Stevenson in a speech in Chicago. He questioned
not the need for intelligence-gathering but the timing of
the flight "on the very eve of the long-awaited summit
conference." He added: "One could say with the cynical
diplomat: 'Sir, it was worse than a lie, it was a blunder.' "

Herter, accompanied by Bohlen, Kohler, and other

aides, flew off to Paris in the President's old plane, the
Columbine, Thursday in midafternoon. He omitted the
usual hopeful statement and left with a short "no comment."

For four days now the United States had seemed to be
threatening to continue the U-2 flights. One voice was
raised in the press questioning the wisdom of this. Col-
umnist Walter Lippmann said the Administration had
"stumbled into an untenable policy which is entirely unprecedented in international affairs.

"To *avow* that we intend to violate Soviet sovereignty
is to put everybody on the spot. It makes it impossible for
the Soviet government to play down this particular incident because now it is challenged openly in the face of the
world. It is compelled to react because no nation can remain passive when it is the avowed policy of another
nation to intrude upon its territory."

On Friday the Pentagon announced that Vershinin,
who had been due to arrive the next day, had called off his
visit because of "unfavorable circumstances." During the
day, NASA announced with a straight face that it had
completed its check of oxygen equipment aboard its U-2
weather planes. The flights would not resume, however,
NASA said, until Lockheed had studied the findings in the
field.

The same day the Pentagon announced, equally dead-
pan, that Strategic Air Command U-2's would conduct
atomic-radiation tests over Argentina May 20–June 15. The
results, it was said, would be made known not only to the
Argentine government but to the world's scientific community.

By the weekend Washington was a city almost empty

of diplomats. The great summit meeting was about to begin in the City of Light.

On Saturday, May 14, Eisenhower called off plans for
filming a brief presummit statement.

At Andrews Air Force Base near Washington, only a
handful of government officials and diplomats were on
hand to see him off. The President walked past waiting
microphones that had been set up in the hope that he might
change his mind and make some farewell remarks.

At the door of his big Air Force jet, the President
turned for an instant, smiled and waved. With Colonel
William Draper, the President's pilot, at the controls, the
gleaming silver and orange plane roared down the runway
and lifted off at 7:20 P.M. The diplomats watched as it
thrust sharply upward at great speed, trailing exhaust
fumes.

Scattered raindrops were beginning to fall at Andrews
as the President's jet became a speck in the darkening
eastern sky.

► 10

The Summit

"I would like to say one more thing about . . . summit meetings . . . you have a room full of people . . . you have a big square table and you have around it as many people as you can crowd, and behind that you have two or three rows of so-called advisers. Everybody is talking at everybody else instead of talking with them."

—Dwight D. Eisenhower, March 30, 1960

The fact is, Eisenhower did not like modern diplomacy.

He would, his intimates knew, much rather have been a head of state in an age when foreign ministers had ultimate authority and could shape the destiny of Europe

Francis Gary Powers at the age
of nine

Shortly before leaving the Air
Force in 1956

The U-2 with glider-like wings almost twice the length of its body

Photographs taken by the U-2's camera from thirteen miles up. Note how the enlargement (*right*) of the circled area shows the word "OPERATIONS"

USAF

The U-2 in flight

Mr Macmillan and President Eisenhower in Paris

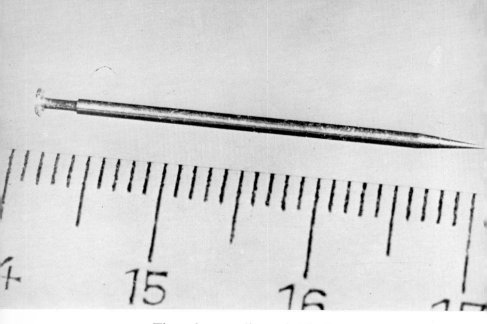

The poison needle carried by Powers

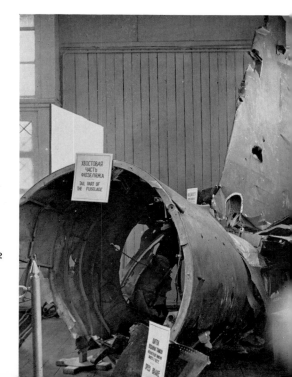

Tail section of the U-2 exhibited in Moscow

Part of Powers's survival equipment

The Destructor Unit of the U-2

Camera Press

БЛОК ПОДРЫВА
С ДИСТАНЦИОННЫМ ВЗВЕДЕНИЕМ

ПРЕДНАЗНАЧЕН ДЛЯ УНИЧТОЖЕНИЯ САМОЛЕТА
ФИРМА БЕКМАН и УИТЛЭЙ.
ПОЛУЧЕН В АВГУСТЕ 1959 ГОДА
(НАДПИСЬ КАРАНДАШОМ)

DESTRUCTOR UNIT
REMOTE ARMED

FOR DESTRUCTION OF THE AIRCRAFT.
BECKMAN AND WHITLEY INC
RECEIVED IN AUGUST 1959
(PENCIL MARK)

The Russian military court

President Eisenhower driving to the Elysée Palace

Khruschev exposing Washington's "cover story"

Photograph of Powers in his flight helmet

Powers's family at the trial

Powers on trial

Associated Pres

Secretary of State Herter and CIA Director Dulles

Associated Press

Los Angeles 1

Left:
Clarence L. (Kelly) Johnson

Right:
Richard M. Bissell, Jr.

Mrs Barbara Powers at a press conference

ander W. Parker and
k W. Rogers

Powers with his family after the verdict

Associated Press

Powers testifying before the Senate Armed Services Committee

beneath gilded chandeliers at the Congress of Vienna.

He wished it were still that way, that foreign ministers wielded the power to negotiate that they enjoyed in the nineteenth century. The President might have agreed with the adviser to Louis XI, who said, "Two great princes should never meet each other face to face, but should communicate through good and wise ambassadors."

But Eisenhower had lost the man he considered his wisest ambassador, John Foster Dulles, in May of 1959. Between then and this May of 1960, the President had found himself walking half-reluctantly, half-hopefully on the road to another summit.

Eisenhower respected Herter but had never enjoyed the same close relationship with him that he had with Dulles. Herter preferred things on paper. With Dulles, the President rarely had to bother with a written document. The two men would sit down together, talk over a situation and one of them might say: "Well, what shall we do about this one?" Eisenhower enjoyed the informality of it.

He had not wanted to be President, to start with. He made it clear in a 1948 letter to a New Hampshire newspaper publisher that military men should stay out of politics. But when, in the spring of 1952, he was persuaded by Henry Cabot Lodge and others that he owed a duty to his country to run, he ran. And once in the White House, he had seen the opportunity that he, a man whose reputation had been built in war, might have to work for peace. In the closing months of his eight-year stewardship, despite three major illnesses, he moved with a new vigor, perhaps because the goal he had set himself seemed in sight.

That goal was: to reach some form of agreement with the Soviet Union that would reduce international tensions,

K

bring about a halt to the arms race and lessen the risk of mutual annihilation.

To achieve this, he was, despite his inclinations, willing to go to the summit once more. His own doubts were increased after Geneva in 1955, where he participated in his first Big Four summit meeting, with Sir Anthony Eden of Britain and Edgar Faure of France. Bulganin's blandishments and the "Spirit of Geneva" had evaporated long before Khrushchev brought the cold war to a new peak in November, 1958.

It was in that month that Khrushchev, now Premier of the Soviet Union, first threatened to squeeze the West out of Berlin. The following January, First Deputy Premier Anastas I. Mikoyan visited the United States for two weeks. The short, mustached Armenian had been to America in the 1930's. Afterward, he introduced Eskimo Pies to the Soviet Union. This trip, he was urging a summit meeting.

Three days later, Charles de Gaulle, that austere, mystical and proud symbol of the glory of France, returned *au pouvoir* as President of the Fifth French Republic. The next month Khrushchev offhandedly invited Eisenhower to visit Russia; the President turned it down but said he would consider a future, formal invitation. On February 16, the Western Big Three proposed that the Soviets join in a foreign ministers conference on Berlin and Germany.

Five days after that, wearing a Russian fur hat, Prime Minister Harold Macmillan of Great Britain flew to Moscow to see Khrushchev. This was the beginning. Now the four heads of state were moving slowly on the path to the summit.

Eisenhower and Foster Dulles had talked privately

for a long time about inviting Khrushchev to this country, as a step toward better relations. But they were reluctant to make the first move. The invitation would be politically sensitive. After Macmillan went to Moscow in February, Dulles told the President: "We're off the hook."

The Secretary of State felt the President was now free to invite Khrushchev whenever it seemed practicable.

But this would push Washington closer to the summit; Eisenhower first wanted some tangible evidence of progress at the foreign-minister level.

The Geneva talks began on May 11, 1959, recessed late in the month for Dulles' funeral, and continued sporadically and unsuccessfully throughout the summer.

In the meantime Eisenhower and Khrushchev were exchanging communications about the possibility of the Premier's visiting America. Early in July a firm invitation went from the White House in great secrecy to Moscow. Just before Nixon flew to Russia for an eleven-day visit on July 22, Eisenhower told him about the invitation.

As part of the agreement, Eisenhower would visit the Soviet Union. He would be given full access to Soviet television to speak directly to the Russian people.

It was to be an unprecedented exchange of visits of the leaders of the two great power blocs in the cold war.

Herter was pressing Eisenhower to announce the exchange before the snarled Geneva talks ended. On August 3, two days before the foreign ministers recessed indefinitely, the proposed mutual visits were announced, bringing a new ray of hope to the world. Late in the month, Eisenhower flew to Bonn, London, and Paris for talks with West German Chancellor Konrad Adenauer, Macmillan, and De Gaulle, in preparation for Khrushchev's visit.

Eisenhower's intimates knew he considered Khrush-

chev shrewd, but not wise, and somewhat lacking in education. (He was amused to learn that Khrushchev had referred to him in private as a mere "water boy.") He had received a two-page cable from Nixon when the Vice-President was in Russia but it had not changed his basic opinion
of Khrushchev.

The President believed that Khrushchev wanted to
visit America because he thought that whenever two big
powers got together they could carve up the map as they
pleased. Stalin and Marshal Georgi Zhukov had spoken to
him in this vein. But he was determined not to make any
deals with Khrushchev. At the same time, he considered
it a good idea to let the Premier come to the United States
and see the country with his own eyes.

He particularly wanted Khrushchev to see his boyhood home in Abilene, to see how a man from the plains of
Kansas could rise to the Presidency. He wanted to take
him on a helicopter ride over Washington to see the small
homes surrounding the city. He wanted him to see labor
on a picket line and the parking lot at Willow Run, because Khrushchev hadn't believed it when Nixon told him
there were sixty million cars in America.

And so, Khrushchev swept into Andrews in mid-Sep-
tember in a big Tu-114 turboprop jet, wearing a homburg
and three shining medals on his black suit. He rode past
restrained crowds in Washington, visited the Lincoln Me-
morial and called Lincoln "a truly great man." He sped,
heavily guarded, through the streets of New York, got
stuck in an elevator in the Waldorf, denied that Russians
drink too much vodka. He whipped off to Los Angeles,
where he watched the filming of *Can-Can,* met Shirley
MacLaine, and went into his famous rage when told he
could not visit Disneyland because of security problems.

He threatened to pick up and fly away home when Mayor Norris Poulson said: "You shall not bury us." But he was laughing soon after in Coon Rapids, Iowa, as farmer Roswell Garst heaved corn silage at newsmen.

And then he was off to Camp David, for the serious part of his visit. There the two leaders walked under oak trees along winding gravel paths. Khrushchev showed an interest in disarmament and relaxed his Berlin stand a bit. The two emerged after three days of talks to issue a joint communiqué. In it, Khrushchev lifted his six-month Berlin deadline and Eisenhower agreed to postpone his visit until spring, when, Khrushchev said, the weather would be better in Moscow.

Khrushchev went home telling his people that Eisenhower "sincerely wanted to liquidate the cold war and to improve relations." For his part, Eisenhower conceded in turn that the Berlin situation "is abnormal." And Khrushchev, he said, had removed "many" of the objections to a summit meeting, despite the lack of progress at Geneva.

Earlier, there had been thought of an October summit, but De Gaulle killed the idea. Eisenhower had little choice but to go along with the French leader, whom he had always considered proud and difficult.[1]

Blocked in his desire for an early Big Four summit, Eisenhower resolved that there would at least be a Western summit in Paris before the year was out. On December 3 he began a nine-nation 20,000-mile trip to Asia, the Near East, and Africa, en route to Paris. He was cheered by

[1] Once, when Eisenhower was NATO commander, he informed De Gaulle he would like to see him. De Gaulle, then out of power, sent word back that as an ex-president of France, Eisenhower should call on *him*. Marshal Alphonse Juin solved the delicate problem. Among the handful of men who belonged to the Order of Liberation were Eisenhower and De Gaulle. Juin arranged a dinner of the group at which the two generals went off into the corner for an hour and a half.

millions in Rome, Ankara, Karachi, Kabul, New Delhi, Teheran, Athens, and Tunis.

The Western leaders met in Paris in mid-December and at Christmas the announcement was made to a world longing for peace on earth: The Big Four would meet in Paris on May 16, 1960.

Earlier, in January, there was a simultaneous United States–Soviet announcement that Eisenhower would visit Russia June 10–19. The President was quail shooting with W. Alton Jones, chairman of the Cities Service Oil Co. (His statement was released in Albany, Georgia, where Francis Powers had met and courted Barbara, while she was a $55-a-week Civil Service secretary at the Marine Corps supply center there.)

As part of the atmosphere of good will now building up, Khrushchev sent gifts to Eisenhower, including a jar of caviar delivered to the President by Soviet Ambassador Mikhail A. Menshikov, known as "Smiling Mike." In return, Eisenhower dispatched a heifer and a bull to Khrushchev by Air Force turbojet.

As the presummit winter wore on, there was a great deal of traveling by heads of state. Khrushchev went off on his own tour of India and the Far East, but his reception was less warm than Eisenhower's. Then Khrushchev flew to Paris to see De Gaulle. Immediately the presummit good fellowship began visibly to dissolve.

On April 2, before leaving Paris, Khrushchev warned that when Moscow signed a separate peace treaty with East Germany, it would void "all rights" of the West in Berlin.

On April 4, Herter delivered a stinging speech in Chicago, attacking Khrushchev's threats to West Ger-

many. Menshikov complained privately that the United
States seemed to be reviving the cold war.

On April 20, Dillon made a speech in New York warning that Washington would not let the people of West
Berlin be "sold into slavery" at the summit. Mikoyan called
the speech "incredible."

The United States was attempting to make clear to
Khrushchev that it would be no easy opponent at Paris.
The lines were hardening. At Baku, on the Caspian Sea,
Khrushchev struck back with his toughest speech of all.
After a peace treaty was signed, he said, the West would
"obviously lose the right of access to West Berlin by land,
water or air." Dillon's speech, said Khrushchev, "positively
reeks of the spirit of the cold war."

Oddly enough, while this tough talk was taking place
on both sides, quiet progress was being made at Geneva,
where two related conferences were running through the
winter and spring. In the disarmament conference, the
Russians continued to balk at inspection and controls, but
the nuclear test ban talks were—after more than a year
and a half—apparently nearing agreement.

From the summit, the West hoped there might come,
at the least, definite moves on disarmament and nuclear
testing, and a general reduction of East-West tensions.
Possibly a stopgap agreement on Berlin might emerge
from the talks, which were envisaged as the first in a
series of East-West summits.

It was against this mixed background of belligerence
and progress, hope and despair, Camp David and Baku,
that the U-2 came crashing to earth on the first of May.
Khrushchev had used it to deliver a series of staggering
blows to the West. Like a swimmer caught in a pounding

surf, Washington had been unable to rally from each
succeeding wave before a new one came smashing down.

Small wonder that Khrushchev, the man who held all
the cards, was first to arrive for the game. His blue-and-
white Ilyushin-18 jetliner streaked into Orly at noon Saturday, a full day ahead of any of the Western Big Three
leaders. The Premier raised his gray fedora as he stepped
down the ramp onto a red carpet. Right behind him came
Malinovsky, resplendent in a light gray jacket and cap,
and blue trousers with red stripes.

Khrushchev smiled only once, when three Soviet Embassy children presented a bouquet of roses to him. The
Premier stepped to a microphone, put on his hat and
glasses and read a mild ten-minute speech. He referred
only obliquely to the U-2 and declared that the Soviet
Union, knowing the world's hopes for the summit, "will
exert all effort to make the conference a success."

Then he marched to his car, followed by Gromyko,
Malinovsky, Menshikov, Valerian Zorin, disarmament ne-
gotiator at Geneva, and First Deputy Foreign Minister
Vassily V. Kuznetsov.

Khrushchev drove to the Soviet Embassy at 79 Rue de
Grenelle on the Left Bank, a white stone palace next door
to a girls' school. He lunched there with Soviet Ambassador
Sergei A. Vinogradov, then drove to the envoy's residence
at Brunoy, fifteen miles southeast of Paris. En route he
stopped for a brief stroll in the woods at St. Germain-en-
Laye. At Brunoy, Khrushchev restlessly skimmed stones
over the lake at sunset.

Eisenhower was next to arrive, landing at Orly at 9:30
A.M. Sunday. He was subdued and businesslike. Unsmil-

ing, he walked down the same long red carpet which Khrushchev had trod the day before.

"The hopes of humanity call on the four of us to purge our minds of prejudice and our hearts of rancor," he said. "Too much is at stake to indulge in profitless bickering." It would be "a pleasure," he added, to meet his "old friends," De Gaulle and Macmillan. He made no mention of Khrushchev.

The French had an automobile waiting for Eisenhower. The Secret Service urged him to take an American car, for security reasons, but the President climbed into the French convertible and rode top down to the residence of American Ambassador Amory Houghton on the Right Bank, at 2 Avenue d'Iena. The Sunday morning crowds were casual but friendly, and the President waved back, apparently in a better mood now.

Just before noon, Macmillan slipped into town, arriving at Orly in a small red propeller plane of the Queen's Flight and dressed like a British country squire on any Sunday in May—suède shoes, a worn gray suit, a cardigan sweater and a soft brown hat.

But Macmillan's airport statement did not match the casualness of his attire. He bluntly warned of the possible "extinction of civilization" and that "all that man has strived to achieve through the centuries could be obliterated almost overnight."

Now the protagonists were all on stage.

About the time Eisenhower was arriving at Orly, Khrushchev was exploring Brunoy. Strolling down a lane, he peeked into a house with its front door ajar. With Vinogradov as interpreter, Khrushchev asked for the owner.

"Monsieur Blondin is outside making hay," a young girl replied.

Khrushchev went out back, found M. Blondin swinging a scythe, and asked to try it. The wiry farmer calmly reported to newsmen later:

"Of course, Mr. Khrushchev has a fair cutting motion, but as he is a stout gentleman, his stomach interfered with his swing."

His hay-cutting over, Khrushchev rode into Paris and called on De Gaulle at the Elysée Palace, on the Rue de Faubourg Saint Honoré, in the heart of the city. Dismounted cavalrymen of the Garde Republicaine formed a double line in the courtyard. They brought their sabers up to their polished golden helmets and the band played ruffles and flourishes as Khrushchev crunched across the white gravel and up the front steps with Gromyko, Malinovsky, and Vinogradov.

Khrushchev spent a noisy hour and ten minutes with De Gaulle. He stormed over the U-2, his shouts[2] echoing through the elaborately appointed chambers of the eighteenth-century palace where Madame de Pompadour once ministered to Louis XV.

Khrushchev left behind a memorandum, in French, in which he demanded that the United States halt the flights, condemn them, and punish those responsible.

The purpose of Khrushchev's visit to the palace, it seemed clear, was to persuade De Gaulle to pressure Eisenhower to meet the Russian's conditions.

Two hours after Khrushchev left the Elysée, Eisenhower and Macmillan arrived there to meet with De Gaulle. It was a gloomy gathering, in view of Khrushchev's

---

[2] De Gaulle later told Eisenhower: "I was obliged to tell him to lower his voice."

demands, which he repeated when he called on Macmillan at the British Embassy later in the afternoon.

The American delegation was studying a copy of Khrushchev's memo, which had been received from the French. It was apparent to the Americans that the summit was in imminent danger of collapsing before it had begun.

Eisenhower was under heavy pressure from Macmillan to announce publicly that the flights would be halted. Herter, as late as Saturday night, had privately assured newsmen there had never been a direct threat to continue the flights. Technically he was right. But with the summit only forty hours away, he still refused to predict to reporters whether the flights over Soviet territory would continue or not.

In Washington, USIA Director George V. Allen (no relation to the President's golfing companion) told a television panel that there had been a terrible "misunderstanding" about what Herter had said on May 9. "He has not said that we are going to fly," said Allen. "He hasn't said one way or the other."

Despite the fact that the meeting was crumbling behind the scenes, neither side initiated any attempt to save it. Khrushchev, American officials later insisted, made no attempt to see Eisenhower. Eisenhower made no attempt to see Khrushchev.

"We have initiated no such meeting nor have we been asked for it," Hagerty told reporters Sunday night. "You must ask Chairman Khrushchev why he has asked for no meeting, that's all I can say. There's been no approach."

As night fell, Khrushchev retired to the Rue de Grenelle and Eisenhower, after a quiet dinner with his son, the Houghtons, and the Herters, went to bed at the residence on the Avenue d'Iena.

Overhead, a five-ton Soviet "spaceship" with a dummy man aboard was hurtling around the earth over New York, Paris, and Moscow. It had been launched early that morning, carefully timed for the summit eve.

Shortly after midnight in Paris, a mysterious order for a combat readiness and communications alert arrived at the Pentagon from Gates, who was at the summit with Eisenhower.

The Defense Secretary had learned of Khrushchev's demands to De Gaulle Sunday afternoon. Convinced that the summit was about to explode, he decided Sunday night to order the world-wide alert of United States military forces. He felt it would be a prudent move to have local commanders stand by battle stations all over the globe.

The Pentagon had various types of alerts, numbered one to five and varying according to whether a practice drill was at hand or the planet was on the verge of war. Gates' message to the Pentagon called for a "quiet" alert on a "minimum need to know" basis. The Secretary of Defense did not, however, specify which number alert he had in mind.

In Washington, the Joint Chiefs of Staff, studying Gates' message, decided the circumstances called for a No. 3 alert. Throughout the night the Pentagon transmitted the order to defense installations.

As word of the alert spread, Defense Department spokesmen were at a loss to explain it. They had not been told about it ("minimum need to know") and were unable to answer inquiries that flooded in from across the country.

In Denver, a commercial radio station broadcast this alarming announcement:

"All fighter pilots F-101 and fighter pilots F-102 . . . Code three alert. Hotcake 1 and Hotcake 6 scramble at Lowry [Air Force Base] immediately."

Newspaper and radio stations throughout the nation were deluged with telephone calls during the night. One family took refuge in the basement.

Gates, setting an example, resisted the enticements of Paris at night and stood by his own battle station at the Ritz. He was in telephonic communication with the unified command outside of Paris. Later in the evening he moved his command post to a front room in Houghton's residence, remaining there most of the night.

Just before sunrise on the East Coast of the United States, a harried Defense Department issued a statement explaining that an alert had been held during the night. It was accurate as far as it went, but failed to note that Gates had ordered it from the summit. That was disclosed a bit later in the day.

Although Gates had not visualized any movement of weapons or troops, the Pentagon announced that both the Continental Air Defense Command and S.A.C. had conducted "limited routine air alert activities." No planes were scrambled, the Pentagon said, and "no personnel were affected, except as local commanders used the occasion to test local personnel-recall procedures."

After ten hours, the Pentagon called it off.

It was dawn in Paris, Monday morning, May 16, when Nixon indicated on David Susskind's television show, "Open End," in New York, that the U-2 flights would continue.

The Vice-President defended the timing of the flight, noting that it had taken place "approximately three weeks before the summit." (It had taken place two weeks and one day before the summit.)

Discussing the U-2 flights, to which he said he had been "privy," Nixon argued they were necessary to protect the United States against "surprise attack."

"Now that is why these flights were made in the first place," he said. "That is why an indication has been made that such activities may have to continue in the future.

"Let's suppose, that as a result of what has happened here, that we say since this flight was discovered, the United States will now announce to Mr. Khrushchev, 'Well, since this plane has been knocked down we're going to discontinue activities of this sort.' Look at the position this puts the United States in and our allies."

Nixon left the studio in Times Square four hours before the summit meeting began at the Elysée in Paris.

Khrushchev was up early for the Big Day. At 7:30 A.M. he emerged from the Soviet Embassy with Vinogradov. Followed by a platoon of Paris gendarmes, who seemed dubious of the venture, the Premier strolled through his Left Bank neighborhood, stepping into the specialty food store of Raymond Balade.

"Good morning, ladies and gentlemen," Khrushchev boomed. He walked about, examining French wine bottles. Then he was off again, patting a girl student on the head, and cross-examining a worker on a cement-mixer.

Across town, Macmillan arrived at the American Embassy residence for an 8:00 A.M. breakfast with Eisenhower. They were closeted for two hours. During the morning the President received word that Khrushchev wanted an hour's postponement of the meeting, which had been scheduled for 10:00 A.M. He also learned that Khrushchev planned to bring Malinovsky and Gromyko, although the first session had originally been planned as a meeting of only the Big Four and their interpreters. In view of the change, Eisenhower asked Gates and Herter to accompany him to the palace.

Just before eleven, the limousines began to arrive, three minutes apart, as diplomatically arranged by De Gaulle. The tall, stern French President greeted each head of state in turn at the main entrance.

Khrushchev, looking solemn, was first to arrive at the 242-year-old palace. De Gaulle escorted him up a double stairway built by Napoleon's brother-in-law and lined with gold palm fronds. The French leader ushered Khrushchev into the ornate second-floor salon, once an intimate dining room favored by Madame de Pompadour and now the site of French cabinet meetings.

Entering the small room was like stepping into the eighteenth century. Four huge French windows let in the soft morning light. The pale green walls were almost entirely covered with rich gold and beige silk in an elaborate flower pattern. A white-and-gold chandelier sparkled overhead. On the left was a black marble fireplace, and a huge tapestry covered half the opposite wall.

Khrushchev and his aides immediately took their places at the far south end of the room at the round conference table covered with green felt cloth. Macmillan was next to arrive. He, too, was escorted upstairs by De Gaulle and sat down directly opposite Khrushchev.

Precisely at 11:00 A.M., Eisenhower and his advisers arrived. Macmillan arose and murmured a word of greeting. But Khrushchev remained seated at the table. The

President did not greet Khrushchev and the Russian gave
no sign of recognition, either. Eisenhower took his place
beneath the tapestry, Macmillan to his left and Khrushchev to his right. De Gaulle sat down across from the
President, his back to the fireplace and the great mirror
above it.

The door was shut. Inside, the atmosphere was cold
and tense. Although their aides were present, the four
leaders were very close together around the table. Eisenhower was no more than ten feet from Khrushchev. To
the men gathered around the table, the room seemed very,
very small.

De Gaulle, as chief of state of the host government,
opened the meeting at 11:01 by asking whether anyone
had a statement.

"*Da*," snapped Khrushchev.

"Yes," cut in Viktor Sukhodrev, the Soviet interpreter.

De Gaulle asked Eisenhower whether he would have
a statement, and the President said he would. Macmillan
declared he might have something to say later on.

As chief of state, Eisenhower outranked Khrushchev
and Macmillan, who were both Prime Ministers.

"We shall hear," De Gaulle began, in his correct,
sonorous French, "from the President of the United
States."

"Just a minute . . . " said Khrushchev. "I asked first,
and I have something to say."

Without waiting for any further permission, the Soviet leader put on his glasses and began to read.

His first words made clear what was coming. "A
provocative act," he declared, "is known to have been
committed with regard to the Soviet Union by the American Air Force . . . a specific espionage mission . . . the

plane was shot down by units of the Soviet rocket troops
. . . these acts, their treacherous nature . . . is incom-
patible with the elementary requirements of normal relations between states . . . and conditions for the fruitful
work of the summit conference."

Khrushchev's face was extremely pale, his hands were
shaking, and he seemed to be in a highly agitated state.
His left eyebrow began to twitch and kept going throughout the conference.

"At first," he went on, "the United States State Department launched the ridiculous version that the American plane had violated the borders of the U.S.S.R. by accident." Later, the United States confirmed that the spy
flights were endorsed by "the President personally."

Khrushchev did not shout, but his voice was excited.

"How is it possible productively to negotiate and ex-
amine the questions confronting the conference when the
United States government and the President himself have
not only failed to condemn this provocative act . . . but
on the contrary have declared that such actions will continue to be the state policy of the U.S.A. with regard to the
Soviet Union?"

Khrushchev was flanked on the right by Gromyko and
on the left by Malinovsky, the only person in the room
who wore a uniform. The Defense Minister gave an impression of enormous physical power. Across the green
cloth of the conference table, one of the United States
officials noticed that Malinovsky was wearing among his
thirty-four medals the white, green and red American
Legion of Merit.

Khrushchev, much better dressed than at Geneva in
1955, talked on, his hands trembling. The American official
noted idly that he wore cuff links, but that none of the

L

other Russians wore any jewelry, not even a wedding ring.

"It is clear," Khrushchev was saying, "that the declaration of such a policy, which can be pursued only when states are in a state of war, dooms the summit conference to complete failure in advance."

De Gaulle listened impassively, an imposing figure between Premier Michel Debré and Foreign Minister Maurice Couvé de Murville.

Macmillan was deeply involved in the success or failure of the conference he had initiated. His eyes were sad now, his face sagging, the droopy eyebrows more pronounced than usual.

Eisenhower was busily making changes in his own notes, penciling in notations on white pieces of paper lying on the table before him. He whispered from time to time to Gates on his left and Herter on his right. Bohlen, sitting behind the President and to the right, was furiously taking notes at a small table, as were the President's personal interpreter, Colonel Vernon Walters, and State Department Russian interpreter Alexander Akalovsky.

"From all this it follows," Khrushchev said, "that the United States government . . . must, first, condemn the inadmissible provocative actions of the United States Air Force . . . secondly, refrain from continuing such actions . . . in the future. It goes without saying that the United States government cannot fail to call strictly to account those who are directly guilty of the deliberate violation by American aircraft of the state borders of the U.S.S.R."

Khrushchev, who does not read speeches well, was stumbling by now, fluffing his words. But he continued: "Until this is done by the United States government, the Soviet government sees no possibility for productive negotiations . . . at the summit. It cannot be among the par-

ticipants . . . where one of them has made treachery the
basis of his policy with regard to the Soviet Union."

The red was rising in Eisenhower's neck. His face was
flushed, his mouth set in anger. Herter feared that the
President was about to erupt.

But Khrushchev was not through yet.

The United States, he went on, must reject its policy
of overflights "and admit that it regrets it." If one administration in Washington did not want peaceful coexistence,
then perhaps another would. "Therefore, we would think
that there is no better way out than to postpone the conference of heads of government for approximately six to
eight months."

As to the President's visit to Russia, "unfortunately"
the Soviet people could no longer receive him "with the
proper cordiality." The visit "should be postponed."

Two black sculptured angels supported candelabra
on each end of the mantel behind De Gaulle. When
Khrushchev had finished, the ticking of the gold clock
between the angels could be heard in the hushed room
overlooking the chestnut trees in the Elysée garden.

Eisenhower, speaking in a controlled voice that
masked his wrath, began reading from the notes before
him. The flights, he declared, "had no aggressive intent
but rather were to assure the safety of the United States
and the free world against surprise attack . . . As is well
known, not only the United States but most other countries are constantly the targets of elaborate and persistent
espionage of the Soviet Union."

For the first time, Eisenhower announced that the
United States intended no further flights over Russia.

He declared: "There is in the Soviet statement an evi-
dent misapprehension on one key point. It alleges that the

United States has, through official statements, threatened continued overflights. The importance of this alleged threat was emphasized and repeated by Mr. Khrushchev. The United States has made no such threat.

"Neither I nor my government has intended any. The actual statements go no further than to say that the United States will not shirk its responsibility to safeguard against surprise attack. In point of fact, these flights were suspended after the recent incident and are not to be resumed.[3] Accordingly, this cannot be the issue . . . I see no reason to use this incident to disrupt the conference."

The President added that he would present a new Open Skies plan to the United Nations. He was prepared to hold separate conversations with Khrushchev "while the main conference proceeds."

When Eisenhower had concluded, Khrushchev responded. He had listened to the assurances of the President of the U.S.A. with some satisfaction, he said. But the question arose from this whether the statement of the President meant that the aggressive aerial incursions against the Soviet Union were merely being stopped for the duration of the conference of heads of government.

No, Eisenhower responded, it was indefinite. Of course, he noted, raising a constitutional point, "I cannot bind my successor."

"Nor am I eternal," Khrushchev shot back. Then he added that the President's statement failed to condemn the inadmissible flights, that it contained no expression of regret and no assurances that such acts would not be re-

---

[3] In May, 1960, the U-2 was flying out of nine overseas bases around the globe. Eisenhower pledged only to end flights over Soviet territory. The same pledge was repeated by Kennedy on January 25, 1961.

peated and that the guilty parties would properly be brought to account.

Speaking honestly, as the representative of a great socialist state, he could not take part in seeking correct solutions for the questions confronting the conference until he had received such assurances from the President of the U.S.A.

De Gaulle, who had had enough by now, interrupted.

He was, the French President declared, being overflown eighteen times a day by the Soviet Sputnik which had been launched only the previous day. Perhaps the Sputnik was taking pictures of the territory of France.

At that, Khrushchev raised both hands high above his head, and declared solemnly:

"As God is my witness, our hands are clean and our soul is pure."

No, Khrushchev added, he would not put a camera in the Sputnik.

That might be the case, said De Gaulle, but the Soviet Union had secured excellent photographs of the far side of the moon. He had seen those.

"*Da,*" Khrushchev conceded, in the Lunik sent by the Soviet Union to photograph the far side of the moon, there had naturally been a camera, as was well known.

France, De Gaulle replied, had nothing to hide. He would let France be overflown freely.

Of course, said Khrushchev triumphantly—by your allies. He would let his own allies fly over the Soviet Union, for that matter.

No, De Gaulle replied icily, he did not say allies. Anyone who was not conspiring and plotting could fly over France, which had nothing to hide.

Khrushchev slipped. He did not give a damn about overflights, he roared.

By now the room was a babble of French, Russian and English as the interpreters tried to keep the pace.

As the bickering went on, Macmillan looked even more distressed, but still remained silent.

Malinovsky said nothing. Only occasionally did Khrushchev consult the beribboned Defense Minister or Gromyko.

Khrushchev kept talking. The overflights, he said, were a matter that deeply involved the internal *"politika"*[4] of the Soviet Union.

The aggressive United States policy of aerial overflights had been made public, Khrushchev said, ignoring Eisenhower's announcement of a few moments before. From this it followed, Khrushchev added, that the government of the United States must issue a public statement not only announcing the suspension of the provocative flights but also condemning them and expressing regret. This was the point in question.

De Gaulle broke in again. There was absolutely no connection between a conference at the summit attempting to arrange a peace, he said, and a minor incident of espionage, something in which all countries engage.

Macmillan now spoke. He deplored the fact that after a long and painful ascent toward the summit, the atmosphere should be so clouded.

What had happened had happened, the Prime Minister said. Surely, all of us knew that espionage was a fact

---

[4] Bohlen, who speaks Russian, thought Khrushchev meant the domestic "politics" of the Soviet Union, which would have been an unprecedented admission for Khrushchev to make. Akalovsky, the official interpreter, thought Khrushchev meant internal "policy," which would be another matter entirely. The word can be translated either way.

of life, and a disagreeable one. Moreover, most espionage
activities involved the violation of national sovereignties.

Mr. Khrushchev had argued that the overflights remained American policy, Macmillan added. Indeed, if
that were the case, he would have understood the Soviet
position. But it was plainly not the case, for the President
had now made it entirely clear that this was not American
policy.

Therefore the conference would not be taking place
under the threat of a continuation of flights of this character by American aircraft. The Prime Minister was grati-
fied that Mr. Khrushchev had not proposed ending the
conference, but merely adjourning it. There was, however, a French saying, which was entirely appropriate:
"What is postponed is lost."

The eyes of the world, Macmillan said feelingly, were
on this room and the men in it. Gentlemen, he appealed,
let the summit proceed with its work, on which the hopes
of all people rest.

It was an eloquent statement, but Khrushchev was in
no mood to be pacified.

Herter spoke only once. He pointed out mildly that it
was unclear from Khrushchev's statement whether he had
withdrawn his invitation to Eisenhower to visit the Soviet
Union.

That sent Khrushchev off on a new outburst. The
Soviet people were not hypocrites. They would not be
able to understand how one could invite the representative of a state whose plane had flown over Soviet territory.

"I don't know what I would say to my little grandson,"
Khrushchev exclaimed.

De Gaulle, counseling moderation, proposed at least
a day's recess to see whether the impasse could be re-

solved. He would, said De Gaulle, stay in touch with the
delegations and decide whether to call another session of
the conference.

Khrushchev interrupted to say he did not consider
this the conference of heads of government. It was necessarily a preliminary meeting to determine whether the
conference could take place. But he would not leave town.

"I do not mind a few more days in Paris under the
chestnut trees," he said.

In the meantime, he announced, he would publish
the text of the statement he had made at the preliminary
conference.

Horrified, De Gaulle and Macmillan tried to persuade
Khrushchev that the decision to publish his blast at Eisenhower was a grave step, to be taken only after mature and
due consideration of the consequences. Khrushchev did
not budge.

Now De Gaulle made no effort to hide his exaspera-
tion with Khrushchev.

You have inconvenienced us, he told him coldly. You
have brought President Eisenhower from the United
States and Prime Minister Macmillan from Britain. Your
own Ambassador came to see us two weeks ago and assured us there would be a summit. You said the same thing
at Orly two days ago. Yet, you knew as much two weeks
ago about the U-2 as you know now.

De Gaulle had finished.

The summit conference of 1960 was clearly over.

It was 2:06 P.M. in Paris. Eisenhower, Khrushchev,
De Gaulle, and Macmillan had been together for three
hours and five minutes. The shadow of a fifth man hung
over the table in the glittering pale-green room in the

Elysée. But never once had any of the participants mentioned his name—Francis Gary Powers.

Khrushchev got up from the round table and marched wordlessly out of the room with his entourage, escorted stiffly by De Gaulle down the double stairway. The Russian was smiling enigmatically, and as newsmen and police crowded around his Zil in the courtyard, he leaned over and clapped his chauffeur on the back. To Russians, a red face is a sign of health rather than embarrassment, and Khrushchev said: "Mine is the only red face. Eisenhower's is white. And Macmillan's has no color."

Upstairs, Eisenhower and Macmillan and the three Western delegations were on their feet chatting and milling about.

The President, who had contained his anger during the meeting, now let some of it escape.

"What kind of apology does that man want?" he was overheard to say.

Macmillan was badly shaken.

De Gaulle and Eisenhower padded slowly down the pale-blue carpeting on the stairway, pausing on the landing before a mirror to speak for a few moments. Then Eisenhower walked out to the courtyard, his face grim. He got into his car with Herter, and James J. Rowley,[5] head of the White House Secret Service detail.

They drove directly to the Embassy residence, where Eisenhower, in the privacy of the rear salon on the ground floor, finally exploded. "That guy" and "that so-and-so" were among the milder terms Eisenhower ordinarily used in referring privately to Khrushchev. Now, disappointed,

[5] President Kennedy named Rowley Chief of the Secret Service on August 1, 1961.

upset, and bitterly angry, he expressed himself in even more uninhibited language.

But he managed to laugh, too, when he recalled the picture of Khrushchev summoning "God as my witness."

The President was joined in this room by Herter, Hagerty, Berding and Bohlen. The five men discussed what should be said to the press. Khrushchev had made it clear he would release his statement, so it was obvious that the United States would have to say something as well.

The world knew nothing yet of the debacle at the Elysée. At the Palais de Chaillot, 2,000 newsmen waited for word. Over the loudspeakers came news that the Russians were on the way to hold a news conference. The reporters were gathered in two hot, noisy conference rooms on the fourth floor, and the television lights added to the heat. At three o'clock, Kharlamov, the Soviet press spokesman, and two interpreters walked onto the stage.

Mopping his brow under the lights, Kharlamov began reading Khrushchev's summit statement in Russian. The translators repeated his words, a few paragraphs at a time, in English and then in French.

The reporters were stunned. They turned to each other, incredulous. "It's over, everything is over," one of them said. Kharlamov finished reading, strode from the building, and drove off in a black limousine, a red flag flapping from the hood.

At 4:40 P.M., Hagerty, Bohlen, and Berding arrived late for the scheduled American briefing. Hagerty read the President's summit statement with the added charge that Khrushchev "was determined to wreck the conference. In fact the only conclusion that can be drawn from his behavior this morning was that he came all the way to Paris with the sole intention of sabotaging this meeting on which so much of the hopes of the world have rested."

Hagerty declined to predict whether the summit conference was over or how long Eisenhower would remain in Paris. He said the President would have refused to go to Russia anyway, and Khrushchev's withdrawal of the invitation saved the President the trouble of turning it down.

Into the night, Macmillan strove desperately to save the conference. In rapid succession, he called on De Gaulle, Eisenhower and Khrushchev. He appealed to Khrushchev to relent and let the summit proceed, but received no encouragement. It was approaching midnight when Macmillan dispiritedly left the Rue de Grenelle.

The Western powers agreed to meet in the morning.

Monday had been tragedy. Tuesday was *opéra bouffe.* It began seriously enough, with a 10:00 A.M. meeting of Eisenhower, Macmillan, and De Gaulle at the Elysée. Macmillan reported on his unproductive session the night before with Khrushchev. Fifteen minutes later they were joined by their foreign ministers.

On the Left Bank, Khrushchev bounded out of the Soviet Embassy to tell newsmen:

"Unless President Eisenhower apologizes and admits America made an aggressive action against the Soviet people, I will return home . . . we Soviets will leave Paris tomorrow afternoon." Gromyko and Malinovsky stood by, looking glum.

But Khrushchev was bubbling over. Where was he heading? "I plan an outing in the country with my friends." Where was he going for the picnic with Gromyko and Malinovsky?

"A military secret," replied Khrushchev, disappearing inside.

A few moments later a Russian official came out and revealed the secret. Khrushchev would drive east out of Paris on Route 4. The Premier's convoy swept out of the Embassy behind a roaring motorcycle escort, down a one-way street against traffic. Deux-chevaux and Dauphines honked offendedly and pulled out of the way.

Eisenhower and Macmillan left the Elysée at eleven and went down the street to the British Embassy. It was hot and the sun beat down on the boulevards. The President and the Prime Minister chatted and drank coffee under shade trees in the garden.

At 11:30 A.M., they left for a drive in the country, heading for the residence of General Lauris Norstad, NATO commander. Eisenhower, in a reminiscent mood, wanted to show Macmillan the home where he, too, had lived as commander of Allied forces in Europe nearly a decade before.

At the same moment, De Gaulle was issuing a formal, written invitation to Eisenhower, Macmillan, and Khrushchev to a three-o'clock meeting at the Elysée "to ascertain whether it is possible for the summit conference to begin." It called for a written reply.

A messenger was dispatched across the Seine to the Rue de Grenelle, but Khrushchev was already out of Paris. The written invitation was a touch that lost some of its nineteenth-century elegance when De Gaulle summoned two motorcycle riders, gave them the document and sent them speeding out of town to overtake Khrushchev.

The Soviet Premier was heading for the battlefield of the Marne, seventy-five miles to the east. Marshal Malinovsky wanted to show him a farmyard near Sézanne where he had bivouacked as a youth in the Czar's army.

The Marshal had been born in Odessa and was a machine gunner at sixteen. He deserted to join the revolution in Siberia and became an officer in the Red Army and a hero of World War II.

En route along a side road, Khrushchev's car was blocked by a fallen tree. He got out, borrowed an axe from the amazed woodman who had chopped it down, and lopped off a three-inch branch.

Then the entourage moved on, stopping briefly at a small café where workmen were having their morning glass of wine.

At this hour Macmillan and Eisenhower arrived at the President's former home in the little village of Marnes-la-Coquette. At 12:10 P.M., after a fast look around the estate, they drove to the city hall. Eisenhower wanted to see the Mayor, since he was an honorary citizen of the village.

When they arrived at the red stone Hôtel de Ville in the center of town, the stout, sixty-seven-year-old Mayor, Jean Minot, was at home preparing for a midday repast commensurate with his importance. A villager spotted the visitors and raced down the street to rouse M. Minot. A moment later, the Mayor, amazingly nimble for his weight class, came running toward the President's car.

"My dear President," the Mayor burst out, "how are you and how is Madame?" Eisenhower grinned, and explained that his wife was in the United States. "I would like you to meet the Prime Minister of Great Britain," he said. The Mayor was delighted to meet the Prime Minister.

Village children were gathering around, and since no

linguists were on hand, the Prime Minister of Great Britain acted as interpreter for the President of the United States.

Macmillan explained in halting Etonian French that the President would like to see the municipal *chambre* where he had been made an honorary citizen.

They spent a few minutes in the city hall, and then returned to the car.

"I regret you cannot come back and see us," the Mayor said, as Eisenhower shook hands with some of the children clustered around the car. Then the Prime Minister and the President headed back to Paris.

At Sézanne, Malinovsky found his old farmyard, now the property of a startled farmer named René Pignard. Nostalgia engulfed the bristle-haired Marshal and he recounted how he had fought alongside Frenchmen, Englishmen, and Americans, but liked the Americans best, "because they seemed more like Russians."

M. Pignard agreed to throw open his barn to Khrushchev for a press conference. Chickens cackled noisily. Cows eyed the Russian leader and shifted uneasily in their stalls. Just then the outriders dispatched by De Gaulle came thundering into the barnyard, sending hay flying.

Khrushchev read the dispatch and gave a quick reply: "I made it clear I will not attend a summit meeting as long as the United States will not recognize that the reconnaissance was perfidy and promises it will not happen again."

But the message must have started Khrushchev thinking that Paris was now the place to be, for he climbed back into his car and headed for the Rue de Grenelle, breaking all speed limits.

. . . .

At 12:25 P.M., in Room C of the Palais de Chaillot, Hagerty held another press conference. He explained that the United States and Great Britain had accepted De Gaulle's invitation for 3:00 P.M. The President and the Prime Minister were out taking a drive at the moment, he said. A reporter asked:

Q. The President and Mr. Macmillan are out riding in the country. Mr. Khrushchev is out riding in the country. Are they going to meet in the country somewhere? (Laughter.)

A. I don't think so. No.

Q. How many makes a quorum for a summit? (Laughter.)

A. Let's wait till three o'clock.

Khrushchev was back at his Embassy by 2:53 P.M., the moment that Macmillan arrived at the Elysée in response to De Gaulle's invitation. The log of what happened next reads like this:

2:55 P.M.: Sergei M. Kudryavtsev,[6] Minister-Counselor of the Soviet Embassy, telephones the Elysée. Khrushchev would like to know whether the meeting due to begin in five minutes was a preliminary meeting to clarify the points of view expressed yesterday—in which case he would attend—or a meeting of the summit conference, in which case he would not attend, since his demands had not been met by Eisenhower.

---

[6] For one year, under the code name "Leon," Kudryavtsev ran the Soviet spy ring in Canada which was exposed by Igor Gouzenko, a cipher clerk in the Russian Embassy in Ottawa. The 1946 "Report of the Royal Commission" that investigated the case identified Kudryavtsev as "the first head of the military intelligence espionage system" that sent back information to Moscow on the atomic bomb, among other matters. A short, balding man with a toothy smile, Kudryavtsev was named Ambassador to Fidel Castro's Cuba in July, 1960.

2:56 P.M. Eisenhower arrives at Elysée, accompanied by Hagerty and Goodpaster.

3:05 P.M. Palace spokesman announces that a meeting has begun without Khrushchev. At this moment the Premier is relaxing in the Soviet Embassy, where he has a suite once used by Russian dukes and princes.

3:20 P.M. Kudryavtsev telephones again. This time he wants to know whether the meeting in progress is a preliminary conference and whether Khrushchev's conditions have been met.

3:25 P.M. On De Gaulle's instructions, a palace official calls the Soviet Embassy to ask for a written reply to De Gaulle's invitation.

3:30 P.M. Soviet Embassy calls back. Mr. Khrushchev wants an answer to his questions and does not intend to answer the invitation in writing.

4:00 P.M. Soviet Embassy calls again and asks when Khrushchev will receive his answer.

4:15 P.M. Eisenhower, Macmillan, and De Gaulle are told of a press statement issued by Khrushchev in which he repeats his demands. Unless accepted, he will not come to the Elysée.

4:45 P.M. The Big Three draft a communiqué which explains that De Gaulle had invited four leaders to the meeting. It added drily: "President Eisenhower and Mr. Macmillan were present. The absence of Premier Khrushchev was noted. President De Gaulle noted that in these circumstances, the planned discussions could not take place."

5:00 P.M. Meeting adjourned.

It had been a day of Keystone Cop diplomacy, but the comic underlay faded by sunset. As each side maneuvered to blame the other, the fact that stood out was that in a world where each bloc had the power to destroy the other, the meeting at the summit had failed.

The next morning was gray and cloudy. The bad weather washed out the President's plans for a helicopter trip to Chartres. Instead, with Houghton for company, he toured Paris in his bubble-top limousine. He visited Notre Dame and afterwards, for half an hour, stood in the darkness of Sainte Chapelle, studying the soaring Gothic glory of its myriad stained-glass windows. Then he returned quietly to the Houghton residence.

He had been scheduled to visit Lisbon on Monday, after the summit ended. Now it was moved up five days. Eisenhower lunched with De Gaulle, attended a farewell session of the Big Three at the palace and prepared to leave for Portugal in the morning.

At the Palais de Chaillot, Khrushchev held an unforgettable press conference, putting on a show that was topped only by his shoe-pounding performance at the United Nations five months later. For two hours and twenty-five minutes, before 2,000 reporters and other spectators, he lashed out furiously at Eisenhower, shouted, waved his arms and gestured. At times his face was livid, at times he beamed. In the course of it, the lights went out and the microphones went dead. The room was steaming.

Applauded at the start, he clasped his hands over his head like a boxer. Then, Russian fashion, he joined in the clapping. When some began to boo, Khrushchev grabbed the microphone and shouted:

"Chancellor Adenauer has sent some of his riffraff!"

A reporter asked why Khrushchev had not protested the U-2 flights when he was with Eisenhower at Camp David.

M

"I will answer that question, with pleasure," Khrushchev said, leaping up with a smile. "When I was talking in Camp David with President Eisenhower, I almost opened my mouth to make that statement. The atmosphere was so convivial, with the President telling me to call him 'my friend' in English, and calling me *'moi drug'* in Russian. And I thought, Why not raise the matter with this friend of mine? But . . . I became apprehensive and I thought there was something stinky about this friend of mine and I didn't broach the subject. It turned out I was right, because when we caught them red-handed, they said they are not thieves, it's just their thief-like policy, that is all.

"This recalls to mind what we used to do in the Donbas when I was a young boy. Whenever we caught a cat in the pigeon's loft, we would take it by its tail and bang its head against the wall and that was the only way it could be taught some sense."

Khrushchev went on and on, finally joking that he must quit or his overworked interpreters would walk out on him. He raised a glass of mineral water, and with a broad wink at the crowd, proposed a toast:

"Vive la Paix!"

Eisenhower stepped into a helicopter at the Invalides at 7:10 Tuesday morning, whipped through departure formalities at Orly and flew to Lisbon, where his spirits revived to the cheers of crowds in the streets. As the President rested in the gardens of Queluz, the eighteenth-century royal palace, Khrushchev was heading home for Moscow, with a stopoff in East Berlin for a speech. Eisenhower was still feeling the bitterness of Paris, however, for when he spoke to United States Embassy employees he said wryly: "Did you see that cartoon not long ago where it says, 'The next speaker needs all the introduction he can get?' Well, I rather feel that way after coming from this last meeting in Paris."

On Friday, Eisenhower flew home. He landed at Andrews at 2:45 P.M. Mamie, tears in her eyes, kissed her husband on the cheek, and the President, his voice husky with emotion, stepped up on a red-carpeted rostrum and made a moving five-minute speech. An airport crowd of 2,000 interrupted five times with cheers.

The President acknowledged them with a tired smile and said: "By our time, it was one o'clock when I arose this morning. After a trip of this kind, you can well understand what it means to me to have this kind of welcome. I am deeply appreciative . . . it truly means a lot to me."

Republican Congressional leaders, Cabinet members, and Allied diplomats were on hand to greet the President, and as he and Mamie drove over the South Capitol Street Bridge into Washington, a fireboat sprayed its welcome and other craft tootled. Workmen waved from dredges along the Anacostia River.

More than 200,000 people were waiting along the route to cheer the President. As he drove down Pennsylvania Avenue in an open car, he passed between two fire trucks, their peppermint-striped ladders forming an arch over the street. From the top was suspended an American flag, and a banner proclaiming:

"Thank you, Mr. President."

Eisenhower had just returned from the most humiliating experience of his public career. The government of the United States had lied, admitted it lied, denied Presidential responsibility, then admitted it, threatened, for all practical purposes, to continue the spy flights, then suspended them. The summit meeting had blown sky-high.

The President had been publicly castigated by Khrushchev and his trip to Russia canceled.

Yet it is not inaccurate to say that the sign on the fire ladders truly reflected the sentiment of the majority of the American people. For they were thanking Eisenhower, not for the summit collapse, but for being Ike, a beloved symbol, for conducting himself with dignity at Paris.

As he rode down Pennsylvania Avenue, his Presidency was nearing its close, the end of a long road from Abilene.

Over the din of the military band, the sound of the drums, one could hear his optimistic dream of a year before: *He'd like to take Khrushchev up in a chopper and show him Washington, all those houses ringing the city. He'd like to show him Abilene, the town where he grew up; he'd like Khrushchev to see how a man from humble beginnings can grow up and become President of the United States.*

Investigation

A FEW DAYS AFTER HIS RE-
turn from Paris, President Eisenhower invited a large
group of Republican and Democratic leaders to lunch at
the White House. It was assumed he wanted to give an
explanation for the summit failure, but the guests were
wary about raising the tender subject.

Finally, Senator Fulbright posed a question delicately.
The Arkansas Democrat wanted to know why the President had taken the unprecedented step of assuming responsibility for the U-2 flight.

For an instant Eisenhower flashed his celebrated
temper.

"Look, Senator," he said sharply, "this is modern-day
espionage. In the old days I could send you out or send
a spy out and if he was caught, disavow him. But what

do you do when you strap an American-made plane to his back, Senator?"

As the other guests maintained an awkward silence, Fulbright stood up to the Presidential fire. He argued that diplomatic intercourse was impossible when the head of a government defied tradition and admitted his implication in spying.

Fulbright left the luncheon determined to get to the bottom of the summit collapse. On May 24 his Senate Foreign Relations Committee voted unanimously to hold hearings to find out: 1) why a U-2 had been sent over the Soviet Union such a short time before the summit, 2) what the C.I.A. was looking for that was so important, 3) who advised the President to take responsibility.

Fulbright had received encouragement from Adlai Stevenson, who broke the presummit political truce on May 19 in a speech in Chicago before Eisenhower's return.

"Premier Khrushchev wrecked this conference," Stevenson said. "Let there be no mistake about that . . . But we handed Khrushchev the crowbar and sledgehammer to wreck the meeting. Without our series of blunders, Mr. Khrushchev would not have had the pretext for making his impossible demand and his wild charges. And let there be no mistake about that either."

The Republicans responded promptly and indignantly. Everett McKinley Dirksen of Illinois, the Senate Minority Leader, insisted it was Stevenson who had "torpedoed" the summit by allegedly recommending concessions at Paris in a prior interview with a French reporter. Senator Hugh Scott of Pennsylvania accused Stevenson of "gross suspicion of appeasement."

It was becoming more than normally difficult to criticize President Eisenhower. It became well-nigh impossible after Khrushchev took a line close to Stevenson's and Fulbright's in a speech to the All-Union Labor Conference in Moscow on May 28.

Khrushchev claimed he had done everything possible to permit the President to extricate himself from the "absurdly stupid situation he had got himself into" with the U-2 incident.

"We even stated," the Premier declared, "that the President was not likely to have known or approved such actions and that hotheads in the Pentagon and Allen Dulles, that professional spy, were apparently to blame.

"But Eisenhower did not take the opportunity offered to him and declared that the spy flights had been approved by him and were taking place with his knowledge. I am still of the opinion that he did not know. But he, as President, found it awkward to admit that he did not know what was going on in his country . . .

"The President will not agree with this, but the whole world knows that he has two duties: one is to play golf and the other is the Presidential duty. Which is more important? The golf is the main one and the Presidential duty is the secondary one."

If the President were a Russian, Khrushchev mused, he might be given a job as "director of a children's home."

"He would not harm children," Khrushchev taunted. "But as head of a mighty state, he is more dangerous and might do a lot of harm . . . The President with his own hands burned the bridges leading to the summit conference." [1]

---

[1] The American Embassy in Moscow reported that Khrushchev had privately expressed bewilderment at the fact the President assumed responsibility for the spy flights. One Embassy dispatch said the Premier broke up the summit out of personal pique at Eisenhower.

It was in the midst of Khrushchev's personal invective that Fulbright held his investigation between May 27 and June 2. The President had privately expressed strenuous misgivings about the inquiry, and the Democratic leadership was exceedingly edgy about appearing to be Khrushchev's advocate in the prosecution of a man of such matchless national popularity as Eisenhower.

Fulbright insisted he was determined to find out what went wrong, but few of his committee members seemed prepared to ask searching questions. One of them, Senator Kennedy, was out campaigning for the Presidential nomination and attended none of the sessions.[2]

The inquiry was conducted with extraordinary Congressional secrecy and restraint. All testimony was taken in executive session. It was edited by Bohlen and Richard Helms of the C.I.A.[3] before a censored version was released page by page to the clamoring press. Then the stenotyped tapes were put through a Shredmaster and obliterated.

Not a word was made public of Allen Dulles' five-and-a-half-hour presentation, which included elaborate maps, charts, and U-2 photographs. One copy of his testi-

[2] Kennedy was already under attack for an off-the-cuff remark on May 17 in Eugene, Oregon, that Eisenhower might have "expressed regrets" at the timing of the May 1 flight.

Prior to the U-2 incident, the Democrats feared that the Republicans would be unbeatable because of the "peace issue." They could imagine Eisenhower going to the summit in an atmosphere of good will, touring the Soviet Union in triumph, and returning just before the political conventions to transfer his peacemaker's scepter to Nixon.

Now, whatever chance there might have been to turn the "peace issue" against the Republicans seemed to have been undercut by Kennedy's remarks in Eugene. During the campaign, Nixon needled him about it in almost every speech. Kennedy could respond only at the risk of challenging Eisenhower's popularity. He chose for the most part to ignore Nixon's barbs and maintain discreet silence in the matter.

[3] Helms, a former newspaperman, succeeded Bissell as the deputy director of C.I.A. for plans.

mony was sealed, bound, and locked tightly in the committee's files. All other recordings were burned.

The basic lines of the Administration's case had been laid down by Eisenhower in his television report to the nation five days after his return from Paris.

"We did hope to make some progress in a summit meeting, unpromising though previous experiences had been," the President said. "But as we made preparations for the meeting, we did not drop our guard nor relax our vigilance . . . It is part of my grave responsibility, within the overall problem of protecting the American people, to guard ourselves and our allies against surprise attack . . .

"I take full responsibility for approving all the various programs undertaken by our government to secure and evaluate military intelligence. It was in the prosecution of one of these intelligence programs that the widely publicized U-2 incident occurred . . .

"As to the timing [so near the summit], the question was really whether to halt the program and thus forgo the gathering of important information that was essential and that was likely to be unavailable at a later date. The decision was that the program should not be halted.

"The plain truth is this: when a nation needs intelligence activity, there is no time when vigilance can be relaxed. Incidentally, from Pearl Harbor we learned that even negotiation itself can be used to conceal preparations for a surprise attack."

Seven witnesses were called by Fulbright: Dulles, his deputy, General Cabell, Herter, Gates, Dillon, Dryden, and Bohlen. Herter's opening statement reiterated Eisenhower's assertion that there had been a "decision" not to halt the flights as the Paris conference drew near.

"The decision not to suspend this program of flights

as the summit approached," Herter testified, "was a sound decision."

Under questioning, however, Herter conceded that there actually had been no specific decision on whether to halt the flights just before the summit. He explained, however, that the "summit conference was very much on my mind as it was on everybody's mind at that time."

The contention of the witnesses was that the entire U-2 affair had been handled properly by the Administration (Dillon said there was "full coordination"), but that Khrushchev had long before decided to "torpedo" the summit because he realized he would not get his way in Paris.

Herter testified that it was "far-fetched" to think his May 9 statement implied that U-2 flights would continue, or that this had something to do with Khrushchev's actions at Paris. The questioning went this way:

Fulbright: But in view of that statement, do you think that Mr. Khrushchev could accept it and continue the conference?

Herter: Yes; I certainly do if he had wanted to.

Fulbright: Do you think our President would accept such a statement from any other power?

Herter: If he wanted to go to a conference? Certainly.

At the press conference in Paris the day the summit collapsed, one newsman had asked Hagerty why, if the flights had been suspended before Eisenhower got to Paris, there had been no announcement of it. Hagerty was unable to give any clear answer.

But a few hours later, newsmen attended a private

briefing for American reporters conducted by Hagerty. Then they filed stories saying the President had given the order to stop flights over Russia on Thursday, May 12, to Twining and Gates. They reported further that the President did not want to reveal his decision under threats against the United States and its allies. He wished to save his announcement for the summit table.

Now, before the Foreign Relations Committee, Herter testified that he "heard" Eisenhower give the order halting the flights on May 12, but he was vague about it.

". . . He did not give the order to me," said Herter. "I think it was through General Goodpaster, but I am not quite certain . . . Allen Dulles was not present and I have forgotten—I think Gates was present."

It proved an elusive subject for the Senate investigators, however, and they were unable to uncover any written evidence of the order. Gates, who followed Herter to the witness stand a few days later, nowhere in the course of his testimony mentioned having received such an order. (In fact, Gates does not recall ever having received it.)

Although Herter argued that Khrushchev had decided to scuttle the summit long before the U-2 flight, at another point he testified that there were no prior indications of this. And he admitted the "U-2 incident was a convenient handle for [Khrushchev] to use to torpedo the conference."

He also testified that had it not been for the U-2 there might have been "some easing of the overall atmosphere" at Paris. An "interim agreement for Berlin" might have been possible and the disarmament "deadlock" might have been broken.

When Fulbright asked what had been learned from the U-2 affair, Herter replied simply: "Not to have accidents."

The committee's hearings were marked by many bitter exchanges between the senators, mainly as to whether a close scrutiny of the events would give aid and comfort to the Communists. The wrangling was censored out, but in the end the committee admitted frustration. It could not determine for sure if a U-2 had ever been grounded for political reasons. And the witnesses refused to reveal the purpose of the May 1 flight.

The final report said the committee was "disappointed that the responsible officials did not see fit to confide in it [the] one piece of information which is crucial to reaching an informed judgment." [4]

The information withheld *was* significant. To those who ran the U-2 program it was important to send the plane over the Soviet Union on May 1 to check the suspected new ICBM site before the summer fog rolled in. But even more pertinent was their attitude toward the U-2 and the summit.

Although the committee was led to conclude that little specific thought had been given to the approaching meeting at Paris, the subject had, in fact, been elaborately explored. But the exploration did not take place at the lofty level of the officials who testified to the committee. It took place within the C.I.A. and the State Department among those to whom the responsibility of actually running the program had been delegated.

These men decided the flights should continue as long as possible. If a *détente* were reached at Paris and

[4] Senator Albert Gore, the Tennessee Democrat, had urged that the secret be disclosed to Fulbright alone, but even that was rejected.

Eisenhower went to Russia, they reasoned, it might be politically impossible to fly the U-2 again—or at least for a critically long period of time.

There had been discussions in the past as to the advisability of halting certain flights at tender moments in international relations. The flights had never been formally suspended in the sense that the President or Herter ordered the cancellation of missions already scheduled. The program did not work that way. Rather, the men who actually ran the program would anticipate political problems in their informal conversations. They would simply refrain from recommending flights at touchy intervals.

"Someone might say, 'We'd better postpone this for a little while,'" one of them explained, "and a flight would be delayed or postponed. Political factors were always considered. Flights were not suspended by order, but flights were suspended for political reasons in an informal way."

For example, the U-2 was kept out of Soviet air space during Twining's visit to Russia from June 23 to July 1, 1956. Similarly, the overflights were halted during Khrushchev's visit to the United States from September 15 to 28, 1959.

But no such suspension was arranged as the summit approached. After obtaining the approval of the State and Defense Departments in mid-April, Bissell took his map to the White House and went over it with Goodpaster. The summit was very much on Bissell's mind and, as Herter testified, everybody's else's. But the President apparently did not consider it.

Sherman Adams, the Assistant to the President from 1953 to 1958, questioned Eisenhower about it, and quoted the President's answer in his book, *Firsthand Report:*

"You're right," the President replied. "I made the decision, just as I have known about and personally approved every one of those flights. When they brought me the plan for this particular flight over Russia, I approved it as one among several within an intelligence policy already adopted. I had no thought of it having any possible bearing upon the summit meeting or on my forthcoming trip to Moscow."

▶12

A Charming Couple

THE ALEXANDER W. PARKERS
of Richmond had two unfamiliar guests for the Fourth of
July weekend at The Homestead in Hot Springs, Virginia. They were a charming couple, Northerners, yes,
but soft-spoken, with the manners of a gentleman and his
lady. New faces were something of a rarity at "The Hot,"
as Virginia's First Families called their mountain resort,
and the couple were the center of curiosity.

"Meet some old friends of mine," Parker said graciously as people stopped by his table in the dining room.
He was a tall, distinguished, and prosperous lawyer, much-traveled in the North and elsewhere. But the charming
couple were not old friends. They had registered at the
hotel under a pseudonym. They were agents of the C.I.A.

They were there to talk about Francis Gary Powers.

Parker had been reached by the C.I.A. circuitously. There was an outside chance that an American might be permitted to defend Powers at his forthcoming trial and someone responsible was needed. Early in June the State Department had approached the Virginia Bar Association and the Bar had nominated Parker, a past president, and his close friend, Frank W. Rogers of Roanoke.

The two Southern gentlemen saw their duty and accepted on June 21. In the intervening weeks they had spent much of their time in Washington, collaborating with C.I.A. and State Department officials on a defense for their fellow Virginian from Pound.

C.I.A. men would hold whispered conferences with them in hotel rooms, then descend by separate stairways to rejoin them at a restaurant. Letters and notes were frowned upon. Communication was by word of mouth— in person or by telephone. It all seemed a bit silly and cloak-and-daggerish, but the lawyers went along, not presuming to judge another man's profession.

The Virginians and the C.I.A. had come to a meeting of minds by the Fourth of July, when Mikoyan disclosed at an American Embassy celebration in Moscow that the pilot would have a public trial.

The Parkers returned the next day to Richmond to meet Barbara Powers. She had been trying to get to Moscow to see her husband and the C.I.A. decided to put her under the Parkers' wing. Notified at the last minute that she was to go to Richmond, Barbara was caught with a depleted wardrobe. She had been whisked out of Adana on equally short notice and had not had time to gather her things.

A Milledgeville department store owner came to her

rescue, opened his shop on Sunday, and allowed her to outfit herself without charge. Mrs. Parker, an impeccably tailored lady, took one look at Barbara's things and knew they wouldn't do. The dresses were bright and gay in a magnolia-South style and there was not a black one among them. Mrs. Parker determined to take Barbara to New York before she left for Moscow and get her some appropriately conservative apparel.

Though a headstrong girl, Barbara followed the Parkers' advice, at least in the beginning. They were impressed by her intelligence but disturbed by what they thought was a lack of restraint. Barbara was impatient with the government's efforts on her behalf and bridled under the C.I.A.'s discipline.

She had never been close to her father-in-law, and now she was particularly annoyed at his freedom to maneuver. Oliver Powers had not been taken into the C.I.A.'s confidence and so he was not subject to their direction. He was free to solicit money for his expenses and his friend Sol Cury, a Norton department store owner, had made a deal with *Life* magazine to pay for their trip to Russia.

But Barbara's expenses and those of her mother, her doctor, and her lawyers were to be secretly paid for by the government. This imposed an obligation to follow the advice of the C.I.A. and the State Department. She was cautioned against public statements and private approaches that might play into the hands of the Russians.

Oliver, on the other hand, could speak his mind and write personal notes asking Khrushchev to release his son.

"If you come to the Soviet Union," came the reply, "I will do everything I can to help you."

N

Two weeks later, on June 13, Oliver received his visa. The next day Barbara decided to take matters into her own hands. She called a press conference at her mother's home in Milledgeville and released the substance of Gary's first letter from prison. If anyone was to be allowed to visit him, her husband had written, she would certainly be the first.

Encouraged by the publicity, Barbara wrote letters to President Eisenhower and to Herter, and sent a cable to Mrs. Khrushchev. Yet, when she appeared at the Soviet Embassy in Washington on July 27, she was politely informed that Moscow still had not answered her visa request.

"It's difficult to get an answer from the Soviet Embassy," Barbara complained. "But it's also difficult to get an answer from our own State Department. I'd like to see them do more than make a request."

On July 30, the Virginia Bar Association, acting closely with the State Department, responded with a cable in her behalf to Khrushchev. It also put in a plea for Parker and Rogers.

"Lawyers of all nations are keenly interested," the cable said, "in observing operation of Soviet Jurisprudence in such an important case. They will not understand why American counsel are not permitted to confer with Soviet counsel before and during the trial. Request prompt word yes or no so can advise attorneys and American public what to expect."

Three days later the Soviet Embassy produced a visa for Barbara. But there was no mention of Parker, Rogers, or John N. Hazard, a Columbia University law professor whose services had been requested by the other two lawyers. Hazard had studied at the Moscow University Law School, spoke Russian, and was an authority on Soviet legal procedure.

Informally he had learned that the Russians had decided against letting a man of his expertise attend the trial. He had also been told that Parker and Rogers stood no chance of gaining admission as counsel for Powers. Over lunch at the University Club, next door to the Soviet Embassy, Hazard advised the two Virginians to change their applications and seek visas as "personal advisers" to Barbara.

The trial interpreter, he joked, would certainly be relieved to be spared the linguistic challenge of translating their Southern drawl into English and then into Russian.

Hazard's information was good. His application was rejected, but Parker and Rogers, following his advice, were admitted as unofficial counsel for Barbara. Now they might be in a position to carry out their central mission for the C.I.A.—to contact Powers even though he was a prisoner of the K.G.B., the Soviet Secret Police.

The lawyers were under C.I.A. instructions to make every effort to secure an interview with Powers. Then they were to question him closely on the Russian claim that his plane had been hit by a rocket at 68,000 feet. They were to try to determine whether, in fact, he had been hit at all and whether his plane had crashed, as the Soviets alleged, or had made a forced landing. Finally, they were to interrogate Powers on why he had not destroyed his plane according to plan.

The highest intelligence authorities in the United States government frankly did not know the answers to

these questions. They had some electronic information
which seemed to cast doubt on the Russian claim, but it
was inconclusive.

American radar on the perimeter of the Soviet Union
had tracked the U-2 from its operating altitude down to
40,000 feet in a slow decline, then watched it spiral down
to 37,000 feet before falling abruptly from the scope.

American intelligence analysts theorized that Powers
had suffered a "flameout," a phenomenon akin to a blow-
out in a gas stove. Because of its unusual fuel, a U-2
had a tendency to "flameout." When it did, the plane had
to be taken down from the oxygen-poor higher altitudes
to the richer air below 40,000 feet, where the engine could
be reignited.

At that point, the American analysts conjectured,
Powers might have dropped within range of Soviet rockets
or fighters. Some antiaircraft specialists in the Pentagon
had credited the Russians with the ability to send air defense rockets to the altitude of the U-2. But Soviet height-
finding radar had been judged to be ineffective above
60,000 feet. At the operating level of the U-2, Russian
rocketmen were presumed to be firing blind. Still, an un-
expected advance in Soviet antiaircraft technology could
not be discounted. Nor could a lucky shot.

The official Russian line was that Powers was the
victim of a direct hit by a single rocket. But even the
Communist press had questioned this version. On May 10,
the Soviet Army publication *Red Star* published a purported interview in which Powers expressed the belief that
an explosion in his jet engine and not a rocket had forced
his plane down.

Two days later *Red Star* ran a clarifying story to the
effect that the U-2 *was* the victim of "a direct hit." But the

same day Radio Moscow indicated the plane had been hit by shrapnel from a near miss, and the next day the *London Daily Worker* reported in a dispatch from Moscow that the rocket did not hit the U-2 but exploded underneath its tail.

Similarly, at Gorki Park during the U-2 exhibit, soldiers claiming to be members of the unit which bagged Powers' plane confided that they had fired a salvo of rockets. And a Soviet officer on the scene said a near miss had disabled it.

Powers failed to destroy his plane as ordered, *Red Star* had suggested on May 10, because he feared being blown up inside it. The ejection mechanism had last been checked in 1956, the article said, and it "would have spared neither the plane nor the flier."

"Powers apparently knew his bosses' habits very well," it continued. "Probably this is why he did not make use of the catapult, realizing what the end would be."

Khrushchev had implied the same thing in the May 7 speech. C.I.A. officials privately disclaimed any attempt to rig the plane against Powers. But the men at the top of the agency knew some U-2 pilots were worried about whether the timing mechanism would, in a tight situation, give them the precious seconds needed to eject safely.

In addition to their covert responsibilities for the C.I.A., Parker and Rogers were also charged with the overt task of preparing a legal defense for Powers.

Working closely with the C.I.A., the State Department, and experts on Soviet law in the United States, they drew up a brief for the pilot's court-appointed Russian lawyer. They argued that Powers, in flying at the lofty altitude of the U-2, no more violated Soviet air space than Russian Sputniks violated American air space. Further, they judged the Soviet failure to protest for so long a period as tacit permission for the flights. Finally, they contended that Powers was flying, not as an individual, but as a representative of the United States government.

Three copies of the brief were mailed to Moscow, one for the Russian lawyer and two for the American Embassy, one of which was to be held for Parker and Rogers until they arrived for the trial.

The government was pleased with the work of the two gentlemen from Virginia, but one of their hill country colleagues was not. To Carl A. McAfee, Oliver's crewcut thirty-year-old lawyer, their approach smacked of futile "how-high-is-the-sky" legalisms. McAfee, a former office boy for Parker, viewed the Powers trial as a preordained drama. The Russians would use it for propaganda purposes and Powers would inevitably be convicted. The only hope was to mitigate the sentence. For that, Oliver's son would have to be portrayed as a simple lad, the victim of large and unfathomable forces.

McAfee's brief for the Russian lawyer was a collection of pictures of the rustic simplicity of Pound. His approach was personal and political. He was one of those rare creatures, a Virginia Republican, and he was treated accordingly by the Eisenhower Administration. He pleaded Oliver's case at the White House to David Kendall, the assistant counsel to the President. And he received a sympathetic hearing from Nixon.

Scores of prominent lawyers offered their services to Oliver, but he stood by the small-town lawyer whose office was above his shoe repair shop in Norton. The two of them would have some noisy arguments but they would always shake hands afterwards. Oliver had a stern loyalty

to his own and he sent McAfee ahead of him to Russia
to plead for his son.

McAfee arrived in Moscow on August 11, six days before the trial. The city was suffering from schizophrenic
spy fever. On the one hand, government propagandists
were treating the Powers trial with restraint. On the other,
they were arousing the citizenry to militant vigilance
against all foreigners, especially Americans.

The day before, Colonel Edwin M. Kirton, the air
attaché at the American Embassy, had been expelled on
charges of trying to take photographs of military installations in Odessa and "actively carrying out visual obser-
vations" from a train near Sverdlovsk.

That day, Robert Christner, a twenty-seven-year-old
Russian-speaking American tourist, was expelled. He had
worn a "suspicious-looking" money belt, had taken pictures of Baku harbor, and had passed around a copy of
Doctor Zhivago.

The next day, James Shulz, the twenty-one-year-old
son of a Methodist minister, was ordered home from a
YMCA tour. He had given away three Bibles.

Oliver and Barbara arrived separately the following
day, Saturday, August 13, flying into Sheremetyevo Airport twelve hours apart. Oliver landed first in a bright
morning sun aboard a British Comet airliner. He was accompanied by his wife, her physician, Dr. Lewis K. Ingram, and Sol Cury.

Ida Powers, twisted by illness and fatigue, walked
slowly and with great pain from the airplane. Asked by a
reporter for her reaction to the trial, she replied huskily:
"I just don't know what to say."

"They are only poor country folk," Dr. Ingram
pleaded. "All this has been a terrible strain on them."

Oliver was irritable and unresponsive. But later, seated in a brown leather armchair in the lobby of the Sovietskaya Hotel, tears in his red-rimmed eyes, he spoke with simple eloquence of a father's agony for his only son.

"I appeal to Mr. Khrushchev," he read from a piece of hotel stationery, "as one father to another, for the sake of my boy. I understand that he lost a son in the war against Germany, fighting with the boys of the United States for the same cause . . . My son is not a millionaire. He is the son of a workingman from a plain American family, like millions of others in your country . . ."

Shortly after Oliver had finished his statement, Barbara flew in from Brussels on a Soviet Aeroflot jet. She stepped from the plane, all in black except for a prim white collar. A bumblebee buzzed about her head and she fended it off wearily as she made her way to a waiting car. She was too tired, she complained, to answer any questions.

"Maybe tomorrow," said Parker, who had accompanied her. "She's taut as a drum."

Barbara had been awake almost the entire way from New York. On the Sabena flight to Brussels, too tense to sleep, she talked the night through, over drinks, with Sam Jaffe, a C.B.S. reporter. She had been thoroughly briefed by the C.I.A. before leaving and a reporter did not fit the official definition of a permissible confidant. But Barbara was tired of the rules and Sam was easy to talk to.

A short way out of New York, three young Americans joined them in the forward compartment. They claimed to be businessmen and tried to make small talk with Barbara. Failing in that, they occupied themselves by closely following her conversation with Jaffe.

There was a two-hour layover in Brussels, but again Barbara declined to rest, insisting that Jaffe continue their conversation in the terminal lounge. The other members of the party took a trip into town—Mr. and Mrs. Parker, Mr. and Mrs. Rogers, Dr. James Baugh, and Barbara's mother, who alternately worried aloud about her daughter and told graphic stories of her work at the State Mental Hospital in Milledgeville.

Barbara and her mother were sharing a ponderously elaborate suite in Moscow at the Sovietskaya. It was on the second floor overlooking the hotel front and next door to Powers' parents. The living room was done in mahogany and blue brocade and a gilt-framed picture of a Soviet destroyer hung on the wall.

Around a bend in the hall were the rooms of Dr. Baugh and the lawyers. Parker decided to put makeshift "traps" in his luggage to see if the secret police were inspecting the rooms. He never found any sign of them. But the C.I.A. was very much in evidence. There were the familiar whispered conferences in his room and the familiar descents by separate stairways to the restaurant.

The principal challenge to their privacy was the press, camped in the hallway. Parker struck a deal: he would consent to a news conference every afternoon and they would keep the hallway clear. Dr. Baugh was able to make his frequent trips to Barbara's room unmolested. That night he gave her a tranquilizer and, for the first time in twenty-four hours, she relaxed into a sound sleep.

Sunday morning, after breakfast, the two family factions held a fifteen-minute strategy session at the hotel before going separately to the American Embassy for separate conferences. They were at odds on most things. But on one thing they agreed: they both wanted to see

Khrushchev and Powers before the trial.

The Embassy could offer little encouragement. It had been repeatedly rebuffed in attempts to gain access to the pilot.

"The farther you stay away from us," it advised, "the better it will be for you."

Back at the hotel, Oliver and Ida Powers withdrew to their suite. But Barbara consented to hold a press conference in the spacious second-floor lobby. She appeared in a brimmed black velvet hat and a black shantung dress with no accessories. A white marble bust of Stalin faced her squarely as she spoke in a low and controlled voice.

"My husband's work and service," she said, "was all part of a program which required orders from the President with Congressional approval. Therefore, I would term him a reconnaissance scout—not a spy—under orders from his own government . . .

"After all, he was simply the pilot of the plane. He never disguised himself. He didn't pretend to be anyone else. He had no intention of murdering anyone or to confiscate anyone's property. All of these things should be taken into consideration."

Why then, a reporter asked, did he sign a confession?

"The fact that he pleaded guilty of being the pilot of the plane whose wreckage they found in the Soviet Union," Barbara replied coolly, "I only feel that it was normal for him to admit it. What else could he say?"

Barbara had given a very impressive performance. Despite her anxiety and the tranquilizers, she so far had managed her affairs with composure and finesse. The lawyers and the government weren't accomplishing anything, she complained. Why shouldn't she try to handle things herself? Parker and Baugh reasoned with her, cajoled her,

threatened her. She was not to be tamed, but she agreed
to stay put and quiet until their meeting with Gary's Russian lawyer the next evening.

Barbara and Oliver and Ida arrived at the Juridical
Consultants' Headquarters on Neglinnaya Street separately and promptly at 5:00 P.M. Monday. They were accompanied by Parker, Rogers, McAfee, and Cury.

A sign out front said: "Citizens bring here their problems on criminal, state, and administrative affairs."

Barbara, Oliver, and Ida brought their problems to
the small pine-walled consulting room of Gary's court-
appointed counsel, Mikhail I. Griniev, a stocky, baldish
little man of fifty-five with a mustache and a wispy
goatee. This was not his first hopeless case. He had been
a defense counsel at Nuremberg and at the trial of Lav-
renti P. Beria, Stalin's Chief of the Secret Police.

Griniev tried to console the family, but he could hold
out no hope for acquittal. Still, within a very few minutes,
the three lawyers were reassured that he would do the
best he could. He was clearly a highly skilled professional
and, alone with them, a kindly man.

The hour-and-a-half conference was mainly occupied
by the efforts of Parker and Rogers to introduce the evidence and line of argument they had laboriously prepared. Griniev listened carefully to their presentation,
but offered not a sign that he would use it at the trial.

Hadn't he received the brief and the questions sent to
him from Washington? Parker inquired dejectedly.

Oh, yes, Griniev replied, smiling thinly and opening
a drawer in his desk. He pulled out the envelope in which
the brief had been mailed and exposed the contents. It
was apparent they had been scarcely read.

Outside the building several hundred Russians

crowded around the family's cars. The government-controlled press had made no mention of their arrival, but word was seeping out through the older and freer channels of uncensored gossip. A few of the Russians muttered and raised their hands. One or two kicked the tires of the cars in the commonplace manner of Muscovites appraising an automobile. On the whole, it was not a hostile crowd, merely curious. The Americans rode back to the hotel without mishap.

On Tuesday, the day before the trial, the family and the lawyers failed in an attempt to see Griniev a second time. And Vladimir Babkin, chief of Intourist's American section, could provide no answer to their request for an appointment with Khrushchev. The Premier, they were to learn later, was vacationing at the Black Sea.

Barbara had sent a desperate telegram to Gary the day before. But she had received neither a reply nor an indication that it had been delivered. Her worst fears were coming to pass. The United States government was impotent. Khrushchev could not be located. She could not see Gary before the trial and, outside the courtroom, might never see him again. He could be shot or sentenced to jail for life and there was nothing she could do about it. Barbara was on the margin of despair as night fell in Moscow on the eve of the trial.

In this forbidding city in this foreign land she had no one but a stranger-friend, a television reporter who had come to record her husband's doom. Through the long evening and the long night, Sam Jaffe drank with her and listened to her anguish. She was beyond consolation.

At three o'clock in the morning, Barbara announced, "I'm going to the prison."

She was not to be dissuaded and Jaffe called a cab.

The girl at the desk checked with the police and called them back. They could go if they promised not to try to get inside the prison.

Gary was being held at Lubianka, the headquarters of the K.G.B. and the central prison for political offenders. It was located opposite "Children's World," the new department store on Dzerzhinsky Square—named for the first chief of the Soviet Secret Police. A massive stone structure, it looked like an office building and had, in fact, housed an insurance company in Czarist days.

Lubianka had once been a hotel, too, but now in the darkness and rain it seemed as if its doors had never been opened, as if they had been sealed shut from the start. The lower-floor windows were barred from the inside and not a light shone from them.

Barbara tried to leave the cab, but the driver warned her against it. Jaffe got out and stood a few feet away. Barbara sat alone and looked at the cold prison walls. She cried, first in sobs and then softly. When she could cry no more, Jaffe took her back to the hotel to await the trial.

►13

The Trial

MOSCOW WAS COLD AND RAINY on the morning of the trial. A dreary sky mocked the gay colors of the Czars—the yellows in the Kremlin and its domes of gold. Across Manezh Square, a fresh coat of Communist paint had been applied to the green and white House of Trade Unions.

Inside, in the gleaming white Hall of Columns, the Stalinist purge trials had been held in the 1930's. There, on Wednesday, August 17, 1960, Francis Gary Powers went on trial for his life. It was his thirty-first birthday.

Outside, the spectators were arriving in a procession of black Zim limousines. From one of them stepped Barbara Powers, stern and poised in her black ensemble. As she emerged the crowd pushed against the restraining barricades of iron piping, hoisting themselves on each other's shoulders for a better view.

From another car came a bent and gray-haired woman with a black shawl over her head in the manner of a Russian peasant. It was Ida Powers, leaning on the arm of her husband, uncomfortable in his city clothes and black bow tie. A crowd of several hundred pressed about them and Oliver had to force a way into the building.

"Don't you worry," he comforted Ida. "They'll know he's a good boy like he's always been. We'll have him back with us soon."

Ida was fearful, but she had started the day by reading the Sermon on the Mount and she determined to take courage from it.

Inside, Barbara greeted them with reserve, taking a seat to Oliver's left in the family's private box at the rear, 150 feet from the front rows where they had expected to be.

Centered over the stage was the Seal of the Soviet Union, bearing a golden hammer and sickle and superimposed on a colored map of the U.S.S.R., ten feet wide. Forty-four gilt and crystal bead chandeliers glistened between the twenty-eight mock-marble Corinthian columns lining the four walls.

There, in the days of the Czars, Pushkin and Tolstoy had taken their leisure when the Hall of Columns was the Noblemen's Club. There, too, after the Revolution, children partied at New Year's and Lenin and Stalin had lain in state.

A theater bell was calling the audience to their red-plush seats. Dark-suited ushers in red armbands were showing the way with an opening-night flourish.

Close to a thousand persons were in the hall, including Khrushchev's daughter Elena. The balcony was full on all four sides, as was the Soviet section on the floor. But across the aisle, the foreign diplomats' section was half empty. Most Westerners had stayed away, perhaps following the lead of Ambassador Thompson, who had declined an invitation. The American Embassy was represented by Richard Snyder, the Consul, and Vladimir Toumanoff, the Second Secretary.

At 10:01, Powers emerged from 108 days of confinement to stand trial. He was led in by two unarmed security guards in olive-drab jackets, blue trousers and red-banded caps. He stared straight ahead into the battery of camera lights and then slowly looked around the hall. Barbara's composure dissolved in tears and she clasped both hands over her eyes. His parents watched without expression. From their box they could see him only in profile. He appeared fit and suntanned, though faintly alien in his blue, Russian-made, double-breasted suit.

He sat in the prisoner's dock on a backless wooden bench. To his right were the interpreters. They would render simultaneous translations in English, French, German, and Spanish. The non-Russian spectators could follow the trial through earphones.

Immediately in front of Powers was Griniev and across from him sat the Prosecutor, Roman A. Rudenko, Procurator-General of the Soviet Union. He was a bald, fleshy-faced man of fifty-three with rimless glasses and a uniform that looked like a railroad station attendant's. Behind him were six glass-topped cases and four tables containing some of the U-2 gear that had been displayed at Gorki Park.

On the stage beneath the hammer and sickle, the Military Collegium had taken their places. The Presiding Judge was Lieutenant General Viktor V. Borisoglebsky of the Red Army, a sad-eyed man with a lopsided mouth. Flanking him were Major General Dmitry Z. Vorobyev, an artilleryman with wavy, receding hair, and Major General Alexander I. Zakharov, a handsome, square-jawed air officer.

They were in identical dress uniforms, blue trousers with red stripes down the sides and dove-gray jackets with red-piped shoulderboards bearing their gold stars. They sat in high-backed wooden chairs with the pretrial testimony spread before them on a long, cloth-draped table in a dozen thick black volumes.

"Defendant," the Presiding Judge commanded, "you are obliged to stand."

Powers got up off the bench and stood stiffly while the indictment was read.

"Accused Powers," Borisoglebsky then demanded, "do you plead guilty of the charge?"

"Yes," Powers replied in his faintly Southern accent, "I plead guilty."

The Presiding Judge turned to Rudenko and asked him to begin the questioning. The Prosecutor was a man in whom the Soviet government placed great trust. He had risen to the pinnacle of his profession by faithfully executing whatever law had been decreed by his superiors. Clever and flexible, he had pleaded critical illness at the Nuremberg trials when he did not feel sufficiently versed in Western procedure to start his duties as chief Russian prosecutor. Denied a stay, he appeared in court on schedule, blandly announcing he had been cured with a miracle drug, created on the spot by Soviet doctors.

Rudenko needed no subterfuge now. He was expert at the legalisms of such a trial and submissive to its higher political purposes. He turned immediately to Powers' es-

o

pionage work with the 10-10 detachment and his spy flight of May 1. The witness replied matter-of-factly and in detail, presenting himself as an obedient switch-thrower rather than a sophisticated agent. Rudenko led him promptly to the crucial Soviet allegation that the U-2 had been hit at a height of 68,000 feet.

"At what altitude," the Prosecutor asked, "was your plane when it was struck by the rocket?"

"It was at the maximum altitude," Powers responded. "At about 68,000 feet."

"Under what circumstances did this take place?" Rudenko pursued.

"I just finished making a turn," the pilot said. "I was flying one minute straight after the turn when I saw, that is felt, a sort of hollow-sounding explosion. It seemed to be behind me. I could see an orange flash or an orange-colored light behind me."

"How did you leave the plane?" the Prosecutor continued.

"I was unable to use the ejection seat," Powers explained, "because of forces originating in the falling plane. I remember that I was at a height of 30,000 feet and I realized that I could not use the ejection seat. So I opened the canopy and loosened the straps. The centrifugal force pressed half of me against the instrument panel while the other half hung outside. I had forgotten to disconnect the oxygen hoses and they held me in. I had to struggle to get out. The parachute opened automatically immediately after I left the airplane. By that time I was at an altitude of 14,000 feet."

"The plane was equipped with a special means of destruction?" Rudenko prompted.

"Yes," Powers replied, "that's what I was told."

"How was this done?" the Prosecutor asked.

"I don't know what would have happened had I pushed the buttons," Powers said. "I was simply instructed to push them."

Why had he been given the poison needle? Rudenko asked.

"In case I was captured, tortured, and couldn't stand the torture and would rather be dead," the pilot said.

"Were you tortured?" the Prosecutor demanded.

"No," Powers replied. ". . . I have been treated very nice."

Rudenko then alluded to the C.I.A. contract. He wanted to know the penalty for disclosing secret information about the U-2 program.

"I don't exactly remember how the wording went," Powers responded, "but it was said that it was ten years' imprisonment and $10,000 fine or both."

The morning session was called to a halt at 1:45 P.M. Parker decided to buy some binoculars so he and Rogers could watch Powers more closely, particularly if the 68,000-foot question were raised again.

The House of Trade Unions had been turned into a veritable market place. In the main lobby downstairs, news vendors were hawking publications in several languages. Some were about the U-2 incident, some about Khrushchev's travels, including his trip to the United States the previous fall.

Just off the main floor, a big buffet had been set up and waitresses in black-and-white dresses were selling coffee, tea, soda pop, salami sandwiches, and sweet rolls.

The heat was oppressive in the unventilated Hall of Columns as the afternoon session got under way at four o'clock. Rudenko asked a few perfunctory questions and then Griniev was given his first opportunity to interrogate his client.

The intent of his defense was clear at the outset. He immediately introduced McAfee's collection of photographs of Pound, and then he steered Powers through a detailed description of his humble beginnings and his working-class family.

No, Powers had never engaged in politics, had never joined a party and had never voted in an election. Yes, he went to work for the C.I.A. to better his standard of living.

"I had wanted to get a job on a commercial airline or some job like that," the U-2 pilot testified. "But I was too old when my term was up [with the Air Force] and not acceptable. So when I was approached and offered a job in the C.I.A. paying approximately the same salary as a first pilot or captain of an airliner, I felt very lucky to get such a job . . .

"It enabled me to pay my debts, live in comparative prosperity and save money for the future in the hope of buying a house and setting up my own business and be independent of my parents."

He had misgivings about renewing his C.I.A. contract, Powers agreed, because the work was "nerve-racking" and "physically exhausting." He was apprehensive about the May 1 flight but "could not refuse" to go.

"It was an order," he explained. "I would have been considered a coward by all of my associates and it would also have meant an unsuccessful completion of my contract."

Was he sorry about the flight? Griniev prodded.

"Well," Powers replied, "the situation I am in now is not too good. I haven't heard much about the news of the world since I have been here, and I understand that as a direct result of my flight, the summit conference did not take place and President Eisenhower's visit was called off. There was, I suppose, a great increase in tension in the world, and I am sincerely sorry I had anything to do with this . . .

"Now that I know some of the consequences of my flight, though I don't know all of them by any means . . . I am profoundly sorry I had any part in it."

With that the trial came to a close for the day, and Powers, waving tentatively to his family, was led back into confinement. The American observers did not believe he had been brainwashed but they felt his perspective might have been affected by long isolation and the clever promptings of his captors.

"That's my boy right down the line," Oliver announced. "Every word was his."

"If he was brainwashed," Parker cautiously concurred, "they did an excellent job of it, because we are convinced that the boy was telling the truth or thought he was telling the truth."

At a news conference in Washington, President Eisenhower agreed that the trial "doesn't show evidence that he has been brainwashed."

The family were cheered by Powers' apparent good health and his alertness under questioning. They were encouraged further by the personal messages he relayed to them through Griniev just after the 5:10 P.M. recess.

"Tell them I am watching them all the time," Powers requested of his lawyer. "And tell my dad that I hardly knew him—all dressed up in that new suit and wearing that black bow tie. Never saw him before in a black bow tie."

He was worried about his mother, though. She looked

strained to him. Perhaps she should stay away the next day.

For their son, Oliver and Ida had some handkerchiefs as a present. They had thought about writing "Happy Birthday" on the note but decided it would be better to say just: "For your birthday, love, Mom and Dad."

The next morning Ida took her son's advice and stayed away from the Hall of Columns. Her place was taken by her daughter Jessica, who had arrived the night before from Washington. As Powers entered the dock at ten o'clock Thursday for the second day of his trial, she and Barbara broke into tears.

He was wearing the same blue Russian suit.

He had slept for nine hours and remained keen under questioning.

Rudenko apparently felt the 68,000-foot question had not been answered to complete satisfaction the day before. He quickly returned to it.

"It was at that altitude of 68,000 feet that you were flying over the area of Sverdlovsk?" the Prosecutor prompted.

"Yes," the witness responded.

"It was at that altitude that you were struck down by a Soviet rocket?" Rudenko half asserted.

"It was at that altitude," Powers corrected cautiously, "that I was struck down by something."

"You say you were struck down by something?" the Prosecutor demanded.

"Why, I had no idea what it was," Powers persisted. "I didn't see it."

Abruptly, Rudenko dropped the line of questioning for good. He settled the issue to the satisfaction of the court, at least, by submitting the report of Major M. R. Voronov, the commander of the Sverdlovsk rocket battery which allegedly hit Powers' plane.

"As the plane entered the firing range at an altitude of over 20,000 meters [65,600 feet]," Voronov's report declared, "one rocket was fired and its explosion destroyed the target."

Rudenko had met with something less than complete success on the 68,000-foot question. He was to find Powers similarly balky on other points during the day. The pilot refused to go along with the contention that his plane bore no identification marks. And he denied that his pistol was designed solely for "noiseless firing at people in attack and defense."

"It was given to me," he declared emphatically, "only for hunting and I took it for that purpose. Unfortunately, nobody but myself knows that I cannot kill a person even to save my own life."

When the questioning veered to political matters, however, Powers seemed more compliant. The Presiding Judge asked him if he felt he had done his "country a good or a bad service" in flying over the Soviet Union on May 1.

"I would say a very bad service," Powers replied.

"Did it occur to you," the Judge continued, "that by violating the Soviet frontiers, you might torpedo the summit conference?"

"When I got my instructions," Powers said, "the summit was farthest from my mind. I did not think of it."

"Did it occur to you," Borisoglebsky pursued, "that a flight might provoke military conflict?"

"The people who sent me should have thought of these things," the witness responded.

"Do you regret making this flight?" the Presiding Judge concluded.

"Yes, very much," said Powers.

When the afternoon session ended at 5:40 P.M., Griniev declared himself pleased. The taking of testimony had been completed and his client had handled himself well. In view of Powers' repentance and repeated expressions of regret, the defense counsel foresaw a lenient verdict the next day.

But Oliver Powers was not wholly satisfied with the day's results. He was disturbed by reports from home that many people were critical of his son's behavior as a witness.

"What do they want the boy to do?" he demanded. "Carry this whole thing himself? You can't send a boy like that up on a thing like this and then let him stand up there all by himself."

►14
►
►

The Verdict

THE HALL OF COLUMNS WAS
filled Friday morning for the concluding speeches of the
Prosecution and the Defense. A capacity house had been
arranged by permitting Russians to occupy the empty seats
in the diplomatic section.

"Comrade Judges," Rudenko intoned swiftly at ten
o'clock, "the present trial of the American spy-pilot Powers
exposes the crimes committed not only by the Defendant
Powers himself, but it completely unmasks the criminal
aggressive actions of the United States ruling circles, the
actual inspirers and organizers of monstrous crimes directed against the peace and security of the peoples."

The Prosecutor was off on a long and declamatory
summation of Powers' testimony about his work for the

C.I.A. The witness doodled on the back of a blue folder as Rudenko went on for an hour and a half.

"Having bought Francis Powers with dollars," the Prosecutor exclaimed, "having made him an accomplice in its foul crimes, the American intelligence service considered in advance the possibility of the failure of the agent and, striving to avoid exposure, tried to convince him of the inevitability of suicide should he find himself alive on Soviet territory . . .

"Here we have the bestial misanthropic morality of Mr. Dulles and company which for the sake of that yellow devil, the dollar, disregards human life . . .

"The material of the trial conclusively proves that notwithstanding all attempts by the American military to stage a quick-change vaudeville with Allen Dulles as producer . . . this is nothing but an espionage hybrid—the offspring of the Central Intelligence Agency and the military intelligence of the U.S. Air Force covered by the NASA fig leaf . . .

"The experience of World War II shows that flights by reconnaissance planes usually preceded air attacks. But if this was so during World War II, in present-day conditions the appearance of scouts is fraught with a much greater danger. . . .

"The Defendant Powers, whose crimes the American intelligence service paid for so generously, is not an ordinary spy, but a specially and carefully trained criminal. All Powers' actions show that he is by no means a weak-willed and blind tool . . . He cannot plead compulsory fulfillment of an order, for, having voluntarily sold his honor and his conscience, the whole of himself for dollars . . . he acted from mercenary and base motives . . .

"It is precisely these Powerses, reared and bred . . . in

the conditions of the so-called free world, who would have been ready to be the first to drop atom and hydrogen bombs on the peaceful earth, as similar Powerses did when they threw the first atom bombs on the peaceful citizens of the defenseless cities of Hiroshima and Nagasaki . . .

"I have grounds," Rudenko boomed in conclusion, "to ask the court to pass an exceptional sentence on Defendant Powers. But, taking into account the Defendant Powers' sincere repentance, before the Soviet Court, of the crime which he committed, I do not insist on the death sentence being passed on him, and ask the court to sentence the defendant to fifteen years' imprisonment."

Powers sat impassively in the dock. But the family reacted as if the Prosecutor had shouted the prosecutor's cry of the 1930's: "Let this mad dog be shot!"

Barbara and Jessica threw their heads into their laps and a gasping sob rose from the family box. Oliver jumped to his feet and looked down at Ida, his hands on his hips.

"Give me fifteen years here!" he shouted. "I'd rather get death."

But he could not be heard over the standing ovation. And the defense counsel was to offer him no solace in his opening remarks.

"I deem it necessary first of all," Griniev said, "to declare that the defense challenges neither the facts of the charges preferred against Powers nor the assessment of the crime given by the State Prosecutor."

But then he began to bring together the mitigating testimony drawn from his client during the questioning.

"The appearance of Powers over the Soviet Union," he argued, "was not a manifestation of his own will, but was predetermined by the will of the aggressive circles behind him, specifically the Central Intelligence Agency of the United States headed by Allen Dulles, in the system of which Powers was a small pawn . . .

"If those who sent him to commit this crime were alongside him, there is no doubt that [he] could undoubtedly expect a considerable mitigation of punishment.

"The witness was frank and truthful," Griniev pointed out. "It is not accidental that in testimony given at the preliminary investigation Defendant Powers said: 'I know that I shall be tried in your court, but if I happen to return home I shall be tried there as well. But this worries me little because I am not likely to return home.' "

Powers' father had been a poor miner and a humble shoemaker, the defense counsel reminded the court. He had shunned the Marxist sins of employing "hired labor" at his shoe shop and marketing the produce of his farm for profit.

The witness was the victim of "mass unemployment in the United States," Griniev declared, alluding to Powers' difficulty in getting a permanent job after college while 1A in the draft. He was so indoctrinated with American "individualism and greed" that he fell "under the delusion that money does not stink."

Griniev asked the court to display the "humaneness" of a powerful and influential nation.

"Offer a sharp contrast," he concluded, "to the attitude toward Man of the masters of Powers—the Central Intelligence Agency, the ruling reactionary forces of the United States who sent him to certain death and wanted his death."

The great Hall of Columns was silent and the Presiding Judge turned to the witness: "Defendant Powers, you have the word for the last plea."

Powers rose to his feet and read a prepared statement:

"You have heard all the evidence of the case and you must decide what my punishment is to be. I realize that I have committed a grave crime and I realize that I must be punished for it.

"I ask the court to weigh all the evidence and take into consideration not only the fact that I committed the crime but also the circumstances which led me to do so. I also ask the court to take into consideration the fact that no secret information reached its destination. It all fell into the hands of Soviet authorities.

"I realize the Russian people think of me as an enemy. I can understand that, but I would like to stress the fact that I do not feel nor have I ever felt any enmity whatsoever for the Russian people.

"I plead to the court to judge me not as an enemy but as a human being who is not a personal enemy of the Russian people, who has never had any charges brought against him in any court, and who is deeply repentant and profoundly sorry for what he has done."

Then, adding a simple hill-country "Thanks," Powers put himself in the hands of the court and the three judges retired to reach a verdict.

At 5:30 P.M., four hours and forty minutes later, the court returned. Powers stood in the dock as Borisoglebsky recited a long summation of the evidence, much in the denunciatory manner of Rudenko.

"The Military Division of the U.S.S.R. Supreme Court," the Presiding Judge at last proclaimed, "holds established that Defendant Powers was for a long time an active secret agent of the U.S. Central Intelligence Agency, directly fulfilling spy missions of this agency against the Soviet Union and on May 1, 1960, with the knowledge of the government of the United States of America, in a specially equipped U-2 intelligence plane intruded into Soviet air space . . . thereby committing a grave crime . . ."

But Borisoglebsky declared the court impressed by "Powers' sincere confession of his guilt and his sincere repentance."

Out of "socialist humaneness," he said, the sentence was being limited to "ten years of confinement with the first three years to be served in prison."

Powers stood motionless in the dock. Except for Ida, the family was standing, too, stunned and tearless. The audience applauded loudly and turned as one to study their reaction. Soviet photographers rushed around them, pushing cameras from all sides. They posed docilely, staring blankly ahead as the spectators filed from the hall. Then, without a word, Barbara, her mother, Oliver, Ida, and Jessica followed a guard up across the stage and into a judge's chamber for their first meeting with Powers.

As they entered, the prisoner was being led in by his guards through another door. He was crying and his arms were stretched out to them. Barbara and Ida went to him. He put his arms around them and they cried together, speechless, for a minute or so.

A table had been prepared with tea and coffee and caviar, but they couldn't eat. They sat down and looked at each other and tried to talk about simple things—whether to sell the car and how to ship the things from Adana.

There were six guards in the room and, at the beginning, photographers, too. The American lawyers had been barred.

Barbara asked Gary if she could join him after his three years in prison were up. He agreed it would be possible but he didn't think it would be good for her to live at some remote factory site.

Powers was still troubled about his mother. He begged her to take care of herself and not to worry about him. He had thought he might be sentenced to death, he said, and he was relieved to have gotten only ten years.

He was concerned about all the publicity, the family reported later, and greatly disturbed about Griniev's final speech. He had known nothing of it in advance, they insisted, and was distressed by its sweeping attack on the United States.

"After all," they said he pleaded, "I'm still an American and I don't want any part of it."

When their hour was up, the guards led Powers from the room and the family returned wearily to the hotel. There, for the first time since their arrival a week before, they were left alone. The Soviet press had turned from the great show trial to the latest Russian space feat. A five-ton "cosmic ship" had been launched that day. There were two dogs aboard and a television camera to enable their masters to watch their behavior.

In Washington, the State Department was denying the implication that Powers would be tried again if he returned home. There was "nothing in his conduct to warrant prosecution," the Department declared, and, in fact, the pilot's full salary would be paid during his entire confinement in the Soviet Union.

President Eisenhower expressed "regrets [at] the severity of the sentence." And Senator Kennedy agreed it was "extremely harsh." But there was a division of opinion in the citizenry.

Martin B. McKneally, National Commander of the American Legion, had little sympathy. He felt Powers "served his country badly" at the trial.

"We are left with the impression," he said, "that there

was more of the mercenary in him than the patriot."

Mrs. Susan Lynch, a New York widow, expressed a parallel sentiment to a roving reporter.

"Honey," she said, "there's no Santa Claus. They don't pay that kind of money for parting your hair down the middle." [1]

But Oliver, told that the sentence could be cut to six and a half years on good behavior, was becoming hopeful about getting his son back even sooner.

The next day, as the American lawyers sat down with Griniev to work out an appeal, Oliver burst into the office, trailed by the dutiful *Life* representative.

"What good is this doing?" he demanded. "He's going to get out in six months. They don't want to feed him any longer."

Griniev stirred as if ready to call off the meeting, but the lawyers managed to usher Oliver and the *Life* man to the far end of the room. Then Griniev explained how the clemency pleas were to be presented to Khrushchev and President Brezhnev.

On Sunday the lawyers drafted an appeal to Khrushchev and Barbara transcribed it by hand on three pages of American air-mail stationery. Rogers took it to the Krem-

---

[1] A more tolerant view was adopted by Red River Dave, a country-western singer. He recorded "The Trial of Francis Powers" to the tune of "The Battle Hymn of the Republic":

In the stately Hall of Columns nineteen-sixty was the year
When young Francis Gary Powers stood before the Russian bear.
They were trying him for spying, o'er the Soviets he flew
In the famous plane, U-2.

Glory, Glory, he's a hero! Glory, Glory, he's a hero!
Glory, Glory, he's a hero who flew for Uncle Sam.

Far across the foreign waters to the State U.S.S.R.
O'er the Lubianka prison shines a bright foreboding star.
In that godless land of Russia, in that vale of endless tears
They gave him ten long years.

lin in the rain Monday afternoon and handed it to a woman attendant at the Tainitsky Gate, where Soviet citizens bring communications for government leaders.

On Tuesday morning the family met with Powers for a second and final time in an eight-by-twelve-foot office in the Supreme Court Building. There was one window in the room, a clock, and portraits of two heroes of the Revolution. Food was laid out again—caviar, ham sandwiches, bottled water and tea. Barbara had abandoned her black ensemble for the first time in Moscow and appeared in a yellow dress.

Promptly at ten o'clock, Powers was led in by two uniformed guards and two plainclothesmen. He was still wearing the strange Russian suit, but he was more relaxed. And so was the family.

"You have one hour," the interpreter announced.

Ida had brought a package containing some candy bars and a New Testament. Oliver opened it and shook the leaves of the Bible to show nothing was concealed inside. But the interpreter made him put it on the desk.

Barbara had brought a copy of President Eisenhower's remarks about Powers and the U-2 at his last news conference. Her husband read it carefully and said he was pleased.

Oliver offered him some money, but he refused it. "You work too hard for your money," he said. Barbara was to take care of that and also send him an electric razor and packages of food and clothing from time to time. One of the Russian attendants suggested winter work gear—sturdy shoes and a parka.

"Don't you worry about me," Powers comforted. "I'm going to be a model prisoner and study Russian and get all the good-behavior time off that I can."

P

"Thirty minutes left," the interpreter said.

Oliver had been asked by the American Embassy to make sure his son was aware he would be receiving full pay during his confinement. The disclosure provoked no great reaction in Powers, but the guards murmured among themselves at the thought of a captured spy making $2,500 a month.

Jessica asked her brother if he wanted a piece of gum. "No," he replied with a smile. "I don't want to get into the habit."

Oliver was worried about the boy's peeling forehead. But Powers reassured: "I had two colds and the Russians treated it with a sun lamp that was too strong."

The conversation had run thin by the time the interpreter cut it off exactly at eleven o'clock. Powers kissed his wife and his mother, and Ida began to cry. Oliver shook his hand and admonished him to "be a good boy."

The family walked to the door together and the women stopped for a moment to wave a last good-by. Oliver kept walking out of the room, suppressing his tears.

Oliver and Ida left for home the next day. They had been advised by McAfee that it would be wiser to wait a bit before pressing their appeal. Barbara and her party stayed behind, hoping to receive an answer from Khrushchev. Parker and Rogers also wanted time to deliver the second appeal to Brezhnev.

They spent most of Tuesday and Wednesday trying to find out where to deliver it, without success. Finally, on Thursday, they secured an appointment at Brezhnev's office. Still, they were not permitted to see the President himself and his subordinates stubbornly insisted they had no authority to take the petition. Exasperated, Parker shoved it at one of the officials, but he quickly put his hands behind his back. The Russian interpreter shrugged his shoulders. The lawyers left the building, put some stamps on the envelope and dropped the appeal in a mailbox at the Metropole Hotel. Returning to the Sovietskaya, they started packing their things for the flight home Friday.

Shortly after 2:00 P.M., Dr. Baugh rushed into Parker's room and reported: "Barbara's been taken away by two guards."

The lawyer's first instinct was to notify the Embassy, but he remembered its warning to stay away except as a last resort. For close to four hours, the two men resisted the temptation to act. But by six o'clock Parker decided he would have to go to the Embassy. He called his car and was about to leave the hotel when Barbara walked in the front door. She had been taken to Lubianka, she explained, for a last visit with Gary.

They had been left alone in a small room for an hour. All of the guards withdrew when Barbara arrived and she assumed she could at last speak freely to her husband. But Gary cut her off sharply with an abrupt motion toward the walls. They talked cautiously for several minutes, mainly about things she might send him.

Then Gary took her hand and she could feel a blunt pin between his fingers. By cupping their hands, he was able to scratch a few letters on her palm with the pin. Barbara phrased a question with guarded allusion to things that had meaning only to them. Gary scratched an answer on her palm.

For the first time in 120 days, they were, in a sense, alone, exchanging the secrets of a man and his wife.

▶ 15

Prison

POWERS HAD BEEN TAKEN TO
Lubianka within hours of his capture and he had been interrogated continuously until the time of his trial. On his
return to the United States, Powers told the Senate Armed
Services Committee the following story:

Twenty or thirty miles southeast of Sverdlovsk he
made a ninety-degree turn to the left. As he settled on his
scheduled course he heard a dull noise like the sharp sound
of a high explosive. It seemed to be outside and it gave a
slight push to the plane. Then a bright orange light surrounded him and after a moment of normal flight the right
wing started to dip.

Powers put the plane back into a level position, only
to find it nosing forward. He drew back on the stick but

felt no control. The plane suddenly nosed over into a violent maneuver and he thought the wings must have torn off.

Then the body flipped completely over and the plane lurched into an inverted spin with the nose high. The sky revolved in front of him and he was thrown forward in the cockpit.

"My first reaction," Powers testified, "was to reach for the destruct switches . . . but I thought that I had better see if I can get out of here before using this. I knew that there was a seventy-second time delay between the actuation of the switches and the time that the explosion would occur. So, after deciding that I had better check and see if I could get out before actuating the switches, I tried to get into position in the ejection seat so that I could use it. In this particular aircraft there isn't much clearance between the pilot's knees and the top of the windshield, and I was being thrown forward, and if I had used the ejection seat at that time, I would have probably lost both legs just above the knees . . .

"I kept glancing at the altimeter as the aircraft was falling and it was going around very fast. I remembered somewhere during this time above the altitude of 34,000 feet that a friend of mine who had had an accident in an aircraft was having trouble getting out of the aircraft, and I remembered him telling me of his experience.

"He said that he told himself that he just had to stop and think, and this entered my mind at the time, so I just stopped struggling and tried to think, and this was the first time that I realized that maybe I could open the canopy, loosen the seat belt and climb out.

"And, along in here, I saw 34,000 feet on the altimeter, and it was still moving very fast.

"I immediately reached up, opened the canopy . . . I opened the seat belt, and I was immediately thrown forward and halfway out of the aircraft . . . I think the only thing that was keeping me in the aircraft was the oxygen hose. If that had not have been fastened, I would probably have gone out right away, I don't know.

"Well, then, I tried to get back into the aircraft so that I could actuate these destructor switches. I couldn't—the G [Gravity] forces were too great and I could not pull myself back over the top of the windshield.

"I tried to reach around underneath. I knew where the switches were. And I couldn't get my hand back underneath.

"Also, somewhere about this time my face plate of my flying suit frosted up completely. That is when it got into the cold air, and all I could see was just the eyes on the face plate about an inch or so in front of my face. I knew that I was well below 34,000 feet.

"I had no idea of what my altitude was. I couldn't get back in the airplane. I didn't know whether I could get those oxygen hoses loose or not. I couldn't actuate the destruct switches.

"So then I decided just to try to get out. I gave several lunges and something snapped and I was floating free. It was almost immediately that the parachute opened, and this surprised me because I hadn't pulled the ripcord . . .

"A short while after that—I don't remember how long —I got to thinking that this chute was set to open at 15,000 feet or lower; that the maximum altitude it would open would be 15,000 feet; so I knew that I could take my face plate off, and not be in danger from the thin air.

"So I removed the face plate, just left it hanging on the hoses that were connected to the suit, and started looking around, and I was still very high—I estimate above 10,000 feet, but I have no idea of the exact altitude.

"There were a lot of thoughts running through my mind at this time, it is impossible to recall them all, but I remembered I had a map in my pocket. I took this map out, looked at it, tore it into small pieces and scattered it in the air.

"I also thought of the coin with the poison pin in it . . . I got to thinking that when I got on the ground if I were captured they would surely find this coin, but maybe with just the pin lying loose in the pocket it would be overlooked, so I opened up the coin, got the pin out and just dropped it in my pocket . . .

"I couldn't tell where I was going to land. There were a lot of wooded areas there, and there was one fairly large one that I would drift toward and then drift back away from, and I was trying to guide the parachute over to this wooded area, but I had no success in that.

"When I got down fairly close to the ground, there was a car I could see on a dirt road. I didn't know what he was doing, but he wasn't going too fast and he seemed to be just keeping up with me, and the closer I got the closer he would get to me. He came to a little village there, turned left out to the outskirts of the village and stopped, and I guess I was maybe 200 feet in the air at this time, and I think it was two men got out of the car . . .[1]

"When I hit the ground I fell down. When I looked up, one of the men . . . was out grabbing ahold of the parachute to try to collapse it. I remember releasing a strap on one side so that the air would spill out of the chute. A

[1] The two men were identified at the trial as Vladimir Surin and Leonid Chuzhakin, drivers at the local state farm. Pyotr Asabin, an Air Force man retired on a disability pension, and a warehouse worker, Anatoly Cheremisin, also took part in the capture.

couple of these men helped me to my feet . . . They helped me remove my parachute harness and the helmet of the flying suit. They took away the pistol and a knife that I had on my parachute . . .

"These men tried to talk to me and I would just shake my head and indicate that I couldn't understand them.

"One of them pointed at me and held up two fingers, and I got the impression that he was asking if there were two of us, and I told him no, just shook my head no, and pointed to myself and held up one finger telling him that I was alone. And then he pointed up in the air and I looked up and saw what I think was a parachute, but I knew that I had no other parachute on board the aircraft . . . (I thought at the time that maybe this explosion was caused by a rocket and, if so, maybe this parachute was used to recover, say, the first stage or something . . .)

"They just talked among themselves, one on each side of me, caught my arm and led me to this car that I had seen earlier. They put me in the car in the front seat next to the driver and with a man on my right, and there were three, I believe, in the back seat. They had loaded up the parachute, and I think my survival pack, in the trunk of the car.

"They started driving through the village and I indicated to them that I would like to have something to drink, so he stopped in front of a house there in this small village. One of the men went inside, brought out a glass of water which I drank . . ."

When the car started up again, according to a Soviet account, one of the Russians wrote the letters "USA" on the dusty dashboard and Powers responded with a nod of his head. He was taken to the local state farm office, where a security officer tried to question him in German. He shook his head to indicate he couldn't understand.

"They searched me here at this building," Powers testified. "They stripped me down to my underwear, went through my pockets, felt along the seams, but they didn't find the needle at this time.

"They called in a doctor. She was a young woman, I would say about thirty years old. I had some scratches on my right leg which she painted and bandaged. They tried to talk to me several times, but I couldn't understand them and they couldn't understand me . . .

"After a two-hour wait they loaded me up in a military vehicle, a little larger than our jeep [and] took me into a fairly large city which I assumed was Sverdlovsk. It was in the downtown area, into a fairly large office building . . .

"There they performed a thorough search and found the needle at this place. I tried to invent a story there that I didn't know where I was, I was off course, but they brought out the packages that I had in my survival pack, or on my person, with maps of the Soviet Union, Russian rubles and several other items that indicated the nature of the mission. It was then that I decided to follow the instructions that I had received earlier and tell them that I was a member of the C.I.A. and the nature of the mission. It was quite obvious that they knew it anyway.

"I think I stayed there approximately thirty minutes. They made a lot of telephone calls. There was a man who spoke English also and asked me several questions, and that is how I found out my story wouldn't hold up . . .

"They loaded me in a fairly large car, limousine type [and] drove to an airfield . . . There was a jet passenger aircraft [and] they made me run up the steps and led me into the front compartment which contained ten seats . . . Through the curtains to the back when the stewardess walked through I could see that there were other passengers in the back, so I suppose it was a regular passenger flight to Moscow.

"During the flight they asked no questions . . . a couple of men played chess. They ate, offered me food but I couldn't eat, and it was during this time that I made up my mind exactly what course I would follow during the forthcoming weeks. I knew that if these people released the news that I was there—I didn't know that they would at the time, but I knew that if they did—that there would be a lot of stuff in the papers in the States, and I also knew that they probably subscribed to every paper we have, and I wanted to make my story as close to what I thought would be released in the papers as possible.

"I think the flight took about three hours. They took me downtown to the building [Lubianka] that I stayed in until September 9th. [When he was moved to Vladimir Prison, 150 miles east of Moscow.]

"There was another search performed immediately upon my arrival at this building. They took all my clothing and gave me other clothing there. There was an interrogation, I would say, within thirty minutes after my arrival there, and there were quite a few high-ranking people, many of them in uniforms, many of them in civilian clothes.

"I don't remember exactly the questions they asked during this time, but I think it was mostly concerned with establishing that I was a member of the C.I.A., or worked for the C.I.A. and the purpose of the flight . . . Rudenko, who was the prosecutor during the trial, was more or less in charge of this interrogation session. He offered me a Chesterfield cigarette. They asked me, I think at this time, what I knew about Moscow; what I knew about Russia; and I told them I knew very little about it.

"They took me to a doctor's office [and] gave me a shot.[2] This was after dark. I don't know what time it was. They immediately took me to a cell . . . It had a solid door with a peephole in it, one window with opaque glass, and bars on the outside of the glass itself."

The next afternoon Powers was taken on a tour of Moscow. The full-scale interrogation was started on the morning of May 3.

"The sessions varied in length," Powers said, "but there were times as much as ten to twelve hours in a single day, several times at night, but, as the time went on, they got shorter and a longer period between the interrogations.

"It was somewhere in the latter part of May that I had a very bad cold, could hardly talk, that they gave the first day off, that I did not have an interrogation."

"On May 2nd," Powers wrote to Barbara in his first letter of May 26th, "I was taken for a tour of Moscow which I enjoyed very much. These people are real proud of their capital city and it is a beautiful city. Another time I was taken to a park [3] to review the remains of my plane. These are the only two times I have been out of this building . . .

"I am getting along as good as can be expected. I get more than I can eat and plenty of sleep . . . I have been treated much better than I expected. For the first week or so I had no appetite at all but I am doing fine now. . . .

"Barbara, I don't know what is going to happen to me. The investigation and the interrogation is still going on. When that is over there will be a trial. I will be tried in accordance with artical [*sic*] 2 of their criminal code

---

[2] The C.I.A. report said the shot "may well have been a general immunization, and there is no evidence of the use of truth serums or other drugs."

[3] Gorki Park on May 17.

for espionage. The artical states that the punishment is 7 to 15 years imprisonment and death in some cases. Where I fit I don't know. I don't know when the trial will be or anything. I only know that I don't like the situation I am in or the situation I have placed you in. . . .

"I want you to know that I love you and miss you very much. I did not realize how much until I found myself in this situation. Not knowing when, if ever, I will see you again, has made me realize how much you mean to me. I have had plenty of time to think since I have been here and plenty of time to regret past mistakes.

"I am sincerely sorry . . . to be the cause of any suffering or pain that you may be having because of the situation that I am presently in. . . .

"You are on your own now and I don't know for how long. Just be careful and maybe we can still buy a house some day. It is a plesant [sic] thought, owning your own house, especially as I sit here in my cell thinking about it."

"Darling," Powers wrote in his second letter on June 28, "I am very sorry for the mess I have made out of our lives. All our planes [sic] and all our hopes seem to have been in vain. Needless to say my life would be very much different if I had it to live over again. What's done is done and there is nothing I can do about it now.

"Stateside life apparently agrees with Eck [their dog]. I can remember how we tried to get him to gain weight before. I suppose he gets better food there. Take good care of him Barbara for he is a fine dog . . .

"Barbara try to keep my mother from worrying too much . . . I have been afraid that my being here might cause her to have another heart attack. I could never forgive myself if I were responsible for that.

"I remember how you used to try to get me to write home more often. I always kept putting it off even though I knew they wanted to hear from me. They deserved a better son than they had. Maybe I can make up for it someway in the future.

"Darling I can't tell you . . . how sorry I am that all this has happened. You also deserved better than this. It seems I have done nothing but hurt the people I love most—I hope that I will have the opportunity to do better in the future, but the future doesn't look very bright . . ."

Powers wrote a third time to Barbara on July 19.

"The trial date has been set for the seventeenth of August," he related. "I sure didn't expect a trial for my birthday . . . I am still taking walks everyday and am getting a fairly good suntan. I would much rather be getting my suntan on a beach somewhere with you. It's the same sun but it look much better before all this happened. . . .

"I am reading 'Gone With The Wind' now and I like it very much. I don't know why I never read it before . . . I have also been given a Bible which I read every day . . .

"The day is almost finished and after I finish this letter I will read a while and then go to sleep. I like to see night come for that means one more day less to wait. Always before, I hated to see each day pass for that meant one day older . . ."

The first few letters bore the return address:

Mr. F. G. Powers
Moscow USSR
Dzerzhinsky St. 2

Later, after the trial, as he was permitted to write more frequently to his wife, parents, and sisters, the return address changed to:

> F. G. Powers
> Box 5110/1 OD-1
> Moscow, USSR

The envelopes were blue and marked the same way each time. Powers wrote the address in Russian on the left side and in English on the right. The return address was on the bottom right and three or four Russian stamps were placed on the upper right. The envelope opened along the right side.

The letters took as much as a month to be delivered. They were written in light-blue ink on four sides of folded air-mail stationery, white and unlined. The writing was small, legible and neatly aligned. The family had no doubt that it was Powers' hand and saw no evidence of censorship.

The letters were concerned largely with personal matters and nostalgic reminiscences. Powers remembered his fondness for fishing as a boy. He was sorry to hear the dogs had turned mean. It was a shame that Roy Stallard, his brother-in-law, didn't catch that white squirrel. His father loved squirrels, he recalled, and kept them at home until the dog got into the cage and killed them.

Never before had Powers fully appreciated the beauty of the Virginia hills. "I suppose," he wrote in March of 1961, "the apple trees are all in bloom now and everything is green there on the farm . . . There hasn't been much sun this winter."

Powers developed an irregular heart beat in prison.

But his father had lived with the same thing for years and his lady doctor assured him it was nothing serious. He was more worried about his mother's asthma. His doctor had suggested a drug and he passed along the name in Russian because he couldn't find out what it was called in the United States. Wouldn't it be wonderful, he reflected, if he could cure his mother from prison. Then his time in confinement wouldn't be a complete waste. Maybe it would help if she got an air conditioner.

He was surprised to hear his father was on television and even more surprised to learn he had given a speech to the Kiwanis Club.

"I wish we could all get together again," he wrote. "Maybe one of these days we can have a big family reunion."

On the morning of May 1, 1961, one year after his fateful flight over the Soviet Union, Powers awoke to find it snowing. It astonished him to see snow in the spring. But it lasted for only an hour or so and melted as fast as it hit the ground.

"I guess that will be the last time this spring," he said. "The days are much longer and the sun is shining more and more."

By then he had been moved to Vladimir prison. It was the showcase jail of the Soviet Union and every ten days inmates were granted a shower, a shave, and fresh underwear and linen.

Powers took two hours of exercise each day and was permitted to go outside when the weather was good. He could receive seventeen and a half pounds of food, clothing and books each month.

"I don't suppose I can complain with the way things turned out," he wrote, "because I expected much worse . . . " but he made it plain in his letters that he wanted to come home to the United States.

Powers was put to work at Vladimir making envelopes and weaving rugs. He had a thirty-three-year-old Latvian roommate and, until the signal was sounded for lights off, they spent much of the evening playing chess. Powers grew very fond of him. He spoke English, German, and Russian, and he was beginning to learn Spanish with the help of books sent by Powers' family.

"I know I will never forget him as long as I live," Powers confided. He hoped to maintain the friendship through letters after his release. The Latvian was a bachelor and longed to get married, have a family, and contribute to society. He was a victim of circumstances, Powers related guardedly, and got into trouble by doing things which seemed right at the time.

A man could have many regrets with so much time to think. He wished he had studied more in college. He didn't get enough out of it and would have done differently if given another chance.

He was pleased with a book on astronomy that the family sent him. "There are many things about the stars and space that I don't know about and didn't think about very much before. But now I am interested in it."

He wasn't doing too well with his Russian. His memory wasn't the best. But he had gotten beyond the stage of "da" (yes), "nyet" (no) and "speechka" (match).

That didn't mean he had any intention of remaining in the Soviet Union. He indignantly rejected the idea when his father sent him a report to that effect which had been published by the *London Daily Mail* in April of 1961.

"I am a citizen of the United States," Powers wrote, "and am proud to be one. I might not like all the policies of the United States Government, but I feel sure there are many millions of people in the United States who disagree with them . . .

"I cannot imagine where the correspondent . . . got his information unless he invented it himself. You may rest assured that I will return home, where I belong and want to be, as soon as I am released. Remaining here has never entered my mind.

"Don't worry about my doing anything or giving any cause for my country to doubt me. It looks as if this British correspondent is trying, for some reason I don't know, to tell the people that I have renounced my country. I would never do this. I was born an American and intend to die an American . . .

"[Patrick Henry] is remembered, much to his credit, for what he said. It looks as if I will be remembered, much to my discredit, for what some correspondent writes even though there is not a word of truth in what he wrote."

An early release was Powers' principal concern and he followed Soviet-American relations closely.

"I want you . . . to write and tell me everything you hear concerning my situation," he said, "whether or not you think it will raise my hopes or cast them down."

Still, he asked his mother not to "worry much about the world situation. There is nothing you or I can do about it."

He personally did not think a war would take place. "The price in lives would be too great."

Powers was saddened by President Kennedy's first

Q

news conference on January 25, 1961. The President disclosed the release of the RB-47 fliers but disclaimed any negotiations for the U-2 pilot.[4]

"I didn't know until I received your letter," Powers wrote to his sister Joan, "that he [Kennedy] said that the U-2 incident hadn't been discussed [with the Russians]. That doesn't look too good does it. There must be reasons and I certainly wish I knew what they were. Well, time will tell I guess."

Later, Powers was deeply disturbed by news that his father had been unable to see the President before he left for his meeting with Khrushchev in Vienna in June of 1961. Oliver couldn't understand why Kennedy wouldn't hear his case and he kept badgering McAfee. At one point, the lawyer told him about a phone call he had received on a recent trip to Washington. Someone purporting to be an attorney claimed he could arrange a White House appointment for $200. McAfee assumed it was some kind of racket that had no connection with the White House.

But taking the story seriously, Oliver recounted it to his son, and Powers wrote back in despair that there now seemed no hope for him. He complained to McAfee that the government didn't seem to be doing anything to help him. But the lawyer assured him that the government, though restricted in what it could do, was trying its best.

Powers seemed to take courage from McAfee's letter.

[4] The RB-47 was shot down on July 1, 1960, while conducting a peripheral snooping mission near the Arctic Circle. Khrushchev charged it had invaded Soviet skies in the vicinity of Novaya Zemlya, an offshore island where the Russians conducted their atmospheric nuclear tests in the summer of 1961. The survivors, Captains Freeman D. Olmstead and John R. McKone, were released several hours before Kennedy's press conference. The RB47 flew out of Brize Norton, England, and, when attacked, was operating in the same vicinity as a U-2 operated while taking peripheral, slant photographs of the Soviet tests series in 1961.

But he kept pressing the family to make it clear to the world that he had no desire to stay in Russia and desperately wanted to go home.

If Kennedy and Khrushchev were waiting to know how he felt, Powers said, tell them "my bag is packed."

►16

Cloak and Dagger

THE LETTER FROM EAST GER-
many bore the usual return address; Eisenacher Strasse,
No. 22, Leipzig.

In his office at 161 William Street, overlooking the
East River, nineteen floors above the shaded canyons of
lower Manhattan, James Donovan tore it open carefully.

It had been waiting for him, on his desk blotter.

Even as he slit the envelope along the side, Donovan
knew that the missive from behind the Iron Curtain
would look exactly like the others. It would be neatly
typewritten, double spaced, in English. The signature
would be in ink, blue ink.

He was not disappointed. The familiar signature read:

"Hellen Abel."

Donovan scanned the letter, and his eyes opened wide.

This one, he quickly realized, was of more than normal interest. But he did not know that it was the beginning of a trail that would lead him to East Berlin, to the murky edges of the Iron Curtain, in an adventure that would rival *The Third Man*.

The letter was dated May 8, 1961.

"Thinking over the question . . ." Hellen Abel wrote, "I remembered of the letter sent to my husband last year by the father of the pilot Powers. I have not read it, but if I am not mistaken, he suggested to my husband that some mutual actions be taken to help his son and my husband be released."

"Mrs. Abel" went on in the letter to seek Donovan's advice. Would an exchange be possible?

Donovan stared at the letter. He could imagine a cobblestone street he had never seen in Leipzig, walking down it until he came to Eisenacher Strasse, the house at Number 22. But who would be waiting for him inside? A gray-haired lady named Frau "Hellen Abel"—or an agent of the K.G.B.?

The junior partner of Watters & Donovan did not know, but he did know exactly what to do with the letter. He put it in an envelope, as he had the others, and addressed it to Lawrence R. Houston, Central Intelligence Agency, Washington, D.C.

The letter was the first key move in a strange game that had opened almost the moment Powers was captured near Sverdlovsk.

The object of the game was to swap Francis Gary

Powers for the alleged husband of "Hellen Abel"—Rudolf Ivanovich Abel, the Soviet master spy then serving a sentence of thirty years in a federal prison.

The players were the C.I.A., and as far as Donovan knew, the K.G.B., in which Abel was a full colonel. The balding, hawk-faced Soviet spy had posed for nine years as an artist-photographer in Brooklyn, not far from Donovan's duplex apartment on Prospect Park West. He had sent back military and defense secrets to Moscow, using all the arcane tools of his profession—a secret radio transmitter, code books, hollowed-out coins and cuff links for transmitting microfilms.

Little was known about Abel. It was believed he had been born in southern Russia in 1902 of a good family. He had joined the Soviet Intelligence Service in 1927, and had entered the United States from Canada in 1948 as Andrew Kayotis. In 1954 he opened a studio at 252 Fulton Street, Brooklyn, under the alias of Emil R. Goldfus. Neighbors knew him as a soft-spoken man who earned a living as a photographer but was actually more interested in his paintings—which were excellent.

Meanwhile Moscow sent Abel an assistant, a lieutenant colonel in the K.G.B., who entered the country October 21, 1952, under the name of Eugene Maki, with a valid American passport. The real Maki had been born near Enaville, Idaho, in 1919 but returned with his parents to Estonia as a child. The agent was actually Reino Hayhanen, a professional spy in the "deep cover" section of the K.G.B. He knew Abel only as "Mark."

When he arrived in New York, Hayhanen followed his instructions and went to Central Park; he found a sign near Tavern-on-the-Green that said "Beware of Horses." He placed a thumbtack on the sign and stood next to it smoking a pipe.[1] It was the signal that he had arrived safely in the United States.

Hayhanen later made contact with Abel in the men's lounge of the RKO Keith Theater in Queens. Normally, to minimize the danger of personal contacts, the two men utilized "dead drops"—secret hiding places—for coded messages and money in Prospect Park, Riverside Drive, Fort Tryon Park and Central Park.

On June 22, 1953, James F. Boslart, a *Brooklyn Eagle* newsboy, knocked on a door to collect his bill and received some change. Later, one of the coins, a 1948 Jefferson nickel, fell apart revealing a microfilm inside. The newsboy turned the coin over to police, who gave it to the F.B.I. Laboratory examination showed a microscopic hole in the "R" in the word "Trust" on the coin. A needle could be inserted to push open the nickel.

But there were no direct leads tying the nickel to Abel until May 6, 1957, when Hayhanen walked into the American Embassy in Paris and defected to the West. He claimed he was en route back to Moscow from the United States, but feared his fate because he had failed in his mission. Four days later, Hayhanen was flown to New York. He gave a description of Abel.

Agents picked up Abel's trail outside the Fulton Street studio on May 28. On June 21 he was arrested by Immigration agents at the Hotel Latham, on East Twenty-eighth Street in Manhattan, where he was registered under the name of "Martin Collins."

Abel was taken to the federal detention center at McAllen, Texas, where United States agents tried to break him. Under tough interrogation, Abel didn't break. He

---

[1] Hayhanen told the K.G.B. before leaving Moscow that he had given up smoking, but they insisted he smoke the pipe in Central Park anyway.

denied everything, would not even admit he was a Soviet
citizen. He laughed at one C.I.A. offer of $10,000 a year
to change sides.

Abel, the highest-ranking spy ever caught in the
United States, was tried in the Brooklyn federal court and
convicted of espionage in October, 1957, despite a brilliant
defense by Donovan, his court-appointed attorney. Donovan charged the government had gained its spy evidence
unconstitutionally, by searching Abel's room after arrest-
ing him simply on deportation charges.

A man of soft, deliberate speech, whose outward control concealed a strong inner drive, Donovan fought hard
at the trial. He lost, but saved Abel from death. The idea
of a spy exchange was bubbling in the back of Donovan's
mind even in 1957. He pleaded to Judge Mortimer W.
Byers:

"It is possible that in the foreseeable future an American of equivalent rank will be captured by the Soviet
Union . . . At such time, an exchange of prisoners
through diplomatic channels could be considered to be
in the best national interest of the United States."

Byers sentenced Abel to thirty years. The Soviet spy
was sent to Atlanta Penitentiary.

At the time of the trial, Donovan had gone to Allen
Dulles, a close friend who had a high regard for him.

"Do you have any Americans you might want to swap
for Abel?" Donovan had asked.

"No Americans," Dulles answered.

But Donovan mentioned the Americans held in Communist China, and suggested a deal under which Abel
be returned to Russia and the Americans given asylum
in India. The C.I.A. director reported back that his
brother, the Secretary of State, opposed a trade.

Donovan fought the Abel case all the way to the United States Supreme Court. Abel's conviction was upheld, but by a 5-4 split decision. The date was March 28, 1960, thirty-two days before the espionage flight of Francis Gary Powers.

At the time of the trial Abel had promised Donovan a $10,000 fee, which Donovan had pledged to three universities.

When he asked for the fee, Abel said, "Write to my wife in Leipzig."

Donovan did, and correspondence began between 161 William Street and No. 22 Eisenacher Strasse.[2]

On June 2, 1960, a month after the Powers flight, Oliver Powers wrote to Abel at Atlanta offering to approach Eisenhower or the State Department to exchange Abel for his son.

Two days later Abel wrote back to Oliver, urging that he contact his wife in East Germany. The Soviet spy also wrote to Donovan in New York suggesting he meet in Switzerland with his "family's" lawyer to discuss the exchange.

The lawyer, Abel said, was Wolfgang Vogel, Friedrichsfelde 113, East Berlin, telephone 55 75 75.

Donovan went back to Dulles, urging that the C.I.A. now consider an exchange. Dulles, reluctant, reminded Donovan of their 1957 conversation.

Nevertheless, the C.I.A. wanted Powers returned to interrogate him on what had happened on the May 1 mission. And Dulles was aware that the K.G.B. might have equally good reasons for wanting Abel.

Unlike Powers, who was basically a pilot of modest

---

[2] Donovan received his fee via Leipzig, and donated $5,000 to Fordham and $2,500 each to Harvard and Columbia law schools.

education, Abel was a professional, a top official of the world-wide Soviet spy network. He was an accomplished artist, an electronics engineer, and spoke five languages, including English, fluently.

"I wish," Dulles told Donovan wistfully, "we had three Abels inside Moscow."

In the weird world of espionage, nothing is ever done directly when it can be done circuitously. The C.I.A. decided that it might be worth exploring an exchange of Powers for Abel. Donovan wrote to Vogel suggesting a meeting.

Donovan left on June 17, 1960, with his wife Mary on what he announced was a "business trip" to London, Zurich, and other international points of interest.

He conferred with the C.I.A. in London and Zurich and gave them a complete itinerary of his trip. But Wolfgang Vogel did not contact Donovan, and the ex-O.S.S. counsel was under C.I.A. instructions not to make a move to contact Vogel.

Nothing happened, probably because the Russians had not yet had a chance to try Powers and reap a propaganda harvest. Donovan returned to New York empty-handed, with little in the way of souvenirs to add to his collection of sword- and gun-canes and his extensive espionage library on the upper floor of his Brooklyn duplex.

But he remained in touch with "Hellen Abel" in Leipzig. In the meantime, Ambassador Thompson had discussed the possible release of Powers in private talks with Khrushchev.

Khrushchev was calm at these meetings. There was no trace of his Paris press conference rage as he discussed the question with Thompson. But he held out little hope that Powers would be released.

Thompson continually pressed to interview Powers in prison, but the Russians would not let anyone near him. There were stirrings on another front, however.

A few days after Kennedy's election in November, two of his advisers, Dr. Jerome B. Wiesner, later named science adviser to the President, and Dr. Walt W. Rostow, later a White House and State Department official, visited Moscow.

The two men, attending the Pugwash conference of scholars, called on Kuznetsov, the First Deputy Foreign Minister, and urged that the RB-47 fliers be returned without Kennedy having to bargain for them. Weisner and Rostow suggested this as the first step necessary for smoother relations. The secret talks paved the way for the release of the two RB-47 fliers five days after Kennedy took office.

On January 1, 1961, just before Kennedy's inauguration Khrushchev told a New Year's party [3] in the Kremlin that he would like the U-2 incident "to become a thing of the past with the departure of the old President."

Khrushchev said Kennedy had taken the position during the campaign that he would have expressed regret over the flight. Khrushchev hoped that "a fresh wind will begin to blow with the coming of the new President."

On January 25, Kennedy announced that Moscow had released the RB-47 fliers. He added: "Flights of American aircraft penetrating the air space of the Soviet Union have

[3] Thompson's teen-age daughter and a friend left the New Year's party early shortly after Khrushchev's toast. The two girls ran down a long flight of stairs pointing to each other and giggling "U-2, you-too." They were later horrified to learn that their voices could be heard at the party.

been suspended since May, 1960. I have ordered that they
not be resumed."

Three weeks later a letter dated February 8, 1961,
arrived at the White House. It was from No. 22 Eisenacher Strasse. "Hellen Abel" was petitioning Kennedy for
clemency for her "husband." The letter mentioned the release of Olmstead and McKone, but did not refer to
Powers.

Eventually, the letter wound up on the desk of Reed
Cozart, pardon attorney of the Department of Justice.
Cozart wrote back and rejected the plea. He said a study
showed no grounds for clemency.

Then, to 161 William St., came the letter of May 8,
1961, in which "Mrs. Abel" revived the idea of an exchange for Powers.

Lying on Donovan's desk blotter that morning, the
letter looked like the others from the outside. In the
upper left-hand corner of the envelope, like all the rest,
was a typwritten return address: "Fr. E. Forster z Hd.
Fr. Hellen Abel Leipzig. N. 22 Eisenacher Str. 24, Germany."

After scanning the contents, Donovan mailed it to
Larry Houston, his old friend from O.S.S. days, who had
become General Counsel of the C.I.A.

As each letter had arrived from "Hellen Abel" it was
relayed by Donovan to Houston. The C.I.A. prepared the
answer for "Mrs. Abel" and mailed the letter back to New
York, where Donovan sent it off to Leipzig. Donovan
could imagine that the same procedure might be followed
by the other side, with "Hellen Abel's" letters being drafted
in Moscow—very possibly at 2 Dzerzhinsky Street.

Less than a month after "Mrs. Abel's" letter in May
—the first indication that a swap might again be of inter-

est to the Communists—Kennedy and Khrushchev met on a rainy weekend in Vienna, June 3 and 4.

Khrushchev raised the U-2 incident several times at Vienna. He repeatedly said he felt Eisenhower did not know about the spy flights, and strongly indicated that he had really wanted Eisenhower to visit the Soviet Union.

One of these occasions was at a lunch at the residence of American Ambassador H. Freeman Matthews. Kennedy raised a glass of 1953 Perrier-Jouet Brut champagne and delivered a three-minute toast to Khrushchev.

The Soviet leader responded with a ten-minute toast. He recalled the U-2, Eisenhower's assumption of responsibility for it, and the cancelation of his trip to Russia. Khrushchev reiterated, champagne glass raised, that Eisenhower had really known nothing about the U-2. He wound up by saying it would now be possible for an American President to visit the Soviet Union. Should Kennedy decide to do so, he would be very welcome in Moscow.

Meanwhile the letters from Leipzig kept coming. "Hellen Abel" wrote Donovan that she had gone to the Soviet Embassy in East Berlin and that they had listened sympathetically to her proposal of an exchange.

With Houston coaching him, Donovan wrote back suggesting that Powers be released, and that Mrs. Abel then petition the President for clemency for her husband. Donovan also received letters, typed, and in German, from Wolfgang Vogel, who still represented himself as Mrs. Abel's lawyer.

At first the C.I.A. did not seem to be too interested in getting Powers back. The initial proposals were that Powers be released in any neutral area, after which Abel would be deported.

In the early autumn of 1961, there was a radical change in attitude in Washington. The C.I.A. seemed much more interested in getting Powers back. Now Donovan's letters to Leipzig raised the possibility of a simultaneous swap.

Donovan believed all along that the Russians wanted Abel back for two basic reasons. First because there was always the possibility that Abel, weary of his prison cell, might decide to talk, and second, because it would help the morale of Soviet operatives all over the world if one of their number was snatched back from a United States federal prison. It might show there was no need to defect, as Hayhanen had done. Finally, Abel would be useful on the "American desk" in the K.G.B.

By November, Donovan became convinced that a deal was imminent. The letters were going back and forth at a faster pace, and Donovan was working closely with Houston. Occasionally he would telephone the C.I.A. to talk to Houston or his assistant, John Warner, or another man named "Mike."

That month the C.I.A. approved a draft of a letter to "Hellen Abel" agreeing flatly to a swap. The letter, Donovan was informed, had been approved by Secretary of State Dean Rusk. It was then sent to Attorney General Robert F. Kennedy, the President's brother, who would have to approve Abel's release from prison if the deal were to be consummated.

Then the case took a strange twist. On November 8, David Brinkley presented a television show over the N.B.C. network in which a man said to be Hayhanen was interviewed. His face was kept in the dark "for his own protection."

Brinkley announced that Hayhanen, after Abel's imprisonment, "was set up in a comfortable house in the northeastern United States under the care and protection of the C.I.A. He came back out of the security briefly for this interview and went back."

Brinkley did not explain why C.I.A. had let Hayhanen out to appear on a nationwide television show. But intriguingly, the program contained two things that might have tended to reassure the Soviets that Abel was well and still untalkative.

In the course of the interview, Brinkley said Abel "to this day" had refused to talk. Hayhanen agreed, suggesting: "I believe he is afraid that his wife and daughter will suffer, from talking, if Russians will know about it."

Amazingly, the N.B.C. program also showed films of Abel in prison. "And this is he—tall, gaunt, walking alone across the prison yard," Brinkley narrated.

Then another shot of Abel was shown: "Colonel Abel now makes his home in the Atlanta Penitentiary," Brinkley said. "He still paints pictures, and here he is showing the warden one of his works, a portrait of President Kennedy . . . To this day he has refused to talk, to say a word, to admit anything even though the evidence against him is undeniable. And to this day the Russians refuse to admit they even know him or ever heard of him."

Most of the nation's press did not seem curious as to how a television network had gotten a camera into a maximum-security prison to take pictures of the highest Soviet espionage agent ever captured on American soil.

But Abel was furious. He wrote Donovan on lined prison stationery, in a neat hand. He declared he wanted Donovan to take immediate action against the Department of Justice for allowing this "invasion of privacy."

Donovan weighed the request. He then wrote back

and advised his client against kicking up a fuss at this delicate moment, when Robert Kennedy was considering his release.

Somehow, Abel seemed to have remarkable sources, even in Atlanta Prison. Once, when Donovan visited him there, he told his attorney: "On your way back, stop off in Washington. I understand they have opened up a new public exhibition at the F.B.I. on my case. Make sure they don't misrepresent anything."

Donovan stopped off in Washington and examined the F.B.I. exhibit. It had just opened.

The secret flurry of new activity over the possible spy swap coincided precisely with a series of moves that appeared outwardly, at least, to relax the tensions between Moscow and Washington that had mounted all summer after the unsuccessful Vienna meeting. (In July, Kennedy had announced that the United States would fight to preserve West Berlin; in August, the Communists sealed the wall dividing East and West Berlin; in September, the Russians resumed nuclear tests and began setting off monster bombs in the atmosphere.)

In October there were signs of a possible thaw. Khrushchev lifted his Berlin deadline at the Twenty-second Communist Party Congress; in November, Alexei I. Adzhubei, Khrushchev's son-in-law, came bouncing up to Hyannis Port, Massachusetts, and interviewed Kennedy for *Izvestia*.

The first week in January, 1962, Donovan's bag was packed and he was itching for word from the C.I.A. to fly to Berlin.

The exchange seemed almost set, with a new element. It now shaped up as a three-way trade, including the release of Frederic Pryor, the young American who had been arrested in East Berlin on August 25, 1961.

The youth's father, Millard H. Pryor, was a wealthy Michigan industrialist and a friend of Defense Secretary Robert S. McNamara.

Pryor had a most interesting lawyer handling his case in East Berlin—Wolfgang Vogel.

Then, just when everything seemed ready for Donovan's departure, there was a disturbing development. On January 20, Lieutenant Milusc Solakov, a twenty-two-year-old Bulgarian airman, crashed his MIG-19 jet near Bari, Italy, six hundred yards from an American missile base. The Bulgarian claimed he was a defector, but newspapers played the story as a Communist U-2 incident. The Italian government was reported ready to try the pilot as a spy. Some papers speculated that the Bulgarian might be traded for Powers.

A C.I.A. representative was on the scene twenty minutes after the crash and before Italian police could seal off the area. No other Americans were allowed in thereafter. Alarmed that the new element might upset the carefully negotiated Powers-Abel deal, high officials of the Kennedy Administration leaked stories that the Bulgarian plane carried no cameras, and that it was not a spy plane.

Finally, late in January, Donovan received authority from the United States government to fly to Berlin. He wrote to "Mrs Abel," and agreed to meet her or her representative in East Berlin.

Donovan was handed a letter from Cozart indicating that Abel's sentence might be commuted under the proper circumstances.

The attorney flew to London, telling his wife he was off on a business trip. He checked into Claridge's, conducted two or three days of normal business in London,

R

then arranged for a cable to be sent to Mrs. Donovan saying he had gone to Scotland. In fact, on February 2 he flew from an R.A.F. base in England to West Berlin in an American Air Force plane.

The same day, the warden at Atlanta received a telephone call from Washington. Fred T. Wilkinson, Assistant Director of Prisons of the Department of Justice, instructed him to be sure Abel had presentable clothing, because he might be brought to New York for routine questioning by federal officials. But he cautioned the warden not to let this fact get around.

In West Berlin, Donovan lived alone for nine days in a house that had been provided for him in the Dahlem section. He had taken a .32 pistol to Germany, but after discussing it with American officials, decided to leave the gun behind when he crossed the Iron Curtain. On all his trips to East Berlin, he carried no identification other than an American passport. Although he was on a mission for the government, he was acting as a private citizen. Once in East Berlin, he was on his own.

Donovan's entry into East Berlin was simple. Despite the sealing of the Berlin wall, the S-Bahn, the elevated railway, had one stop in East Berlin. Donovan got on it in West Berlin and got off on the other side of the Iron Curtain. He then had to make his way past four East German checkpoints.

He found a magic phrase for slipping through. He simply announced gruffly to the East German police, in German: "I have an appointment at the Soviet Embassy."

As the days passed, Donovan learned to deliver his lines at the checkpoints with more authority. The East German police would salute smartly and let him through.

Donovan's Soviet contact was Ivan Shishkin, the sec-

ond secretary of the Russian Embassy. During their negotiations Donovan spoke some English and some German
with Shishkin, a six-foot-three handsome man who played
volleyball for relaxation—and was suspected of being the
Soviet espionage chief of Western Europe.

Once the Russians produced a woman who purported
to be "Hellen Abel." Donovan, after speaking to her, was
convinced she was a German character actress made up for
the part. He also met a huge man introduced as Abel's
"Cousin Drews."

The hulking, silent "Cousin Drews" tailed Donovan
wherever he went in East Berlin. To Donovan he appeared
to be of Slavic rather than German origin.

Each day, after Donovan returned from East Berlin
and his dealings with Shishkin, he would dial a special
phone number and say: "Jim D. is back." He then went to
the crowded Golden City bar at the Hilton Hotel. There
his C.I.A. contact would drift in and receive Donovan's
report on the day's developments. The report was then
cabled to the White House.

As the delicate negotiations proceeded, Donovan met
another of his correspondents in East Germany, Herr
Vogel. The East German Communist attorney and the
Brooklyn Irishman did not get on well, but Donovan managed to suppress his distaste for Herr Vogel in the interests of arranging the exchange.

In West Berlin, Donovan conferred several times on
the progress of his secret mission with General Lucius D.
Clay, Kennedy's personal representative in Berlin. He also
talked with Major General Albert Watson II, command-
ant of United States forces in Berlin, and Allan Lightner.

After days of trips back and forth between West and
East Berlin, and endless rounds of conferences with Shish-

kin, Vogel, and Clay, the deal appeared to be nearing completion.

In Washington, just before leaving on a world trip, Robert Kennedy signed the necessary papers to deport Abel. The President signed an order commuting Abel's sentence, effective the moment of the exchange. It provided that Abel must never return to the United States.

On Tuesday, February 6, Wilkinson was notified that he would probably have to move into action. He had been warden at Atlanta while Abel was there and knew him intimately. He was let in on the secret of the exchange negotiations early in January.

At seven o'clock that night he called the warden in Atlanta again and instructed him to move Abel to New York. Wilkinson, familiar with the prison's routine, told the warden to wait until after the midnight count. There would be some milling about in the cellblocks at that time and a prisoner could be removed without its being too obvious.

Wilkinson and Noah L. Aldredge, Chief of Custodial Service of the Bureau of Prisons, took a train to New York that afternoon and checked into the Henry Hudson Hotel on West Fifty-seventh Street to wait.

At 12:30 A.M. Wednesday, February 7, Abel got dressed and was quietly removed from his cell at Atlanta in the custody of Earl Peck, senior officer at the prison. Orders were issued that Abel's cellmates and two other prison friends were to be barred from having visitors for a few days.

The other passengers aboard the commercial jet liner that left Atlanta at 2:00 A.M. for Idlewild paid no particular attention to the husky man and his thinner companion who seemed always to stay by his side.

At the Henry Hudson, Wilkinson received word that

"the package" was in the air. This was how Abel was referred to in the secret dealings—never by name. The prison
official then called the Federal House of Detention, at 427
West Street, Manhattan, and told the lieutenant on duty
that "a man" would be arriving at dawn. He instructed him
to put the man in one of the three maximum-security cells.

Abel landed at Idlewild at 4:30 A.M. and was taken
by car directly to the detention headquarters on West
Street. He knew something unusual was happening, but
was not sure what.

On the other side of the world, at 7:30 P.M. Wednesday night, a group of men and an interpreter arrived without warning at Powers' cell at Vladimir Prison. They asked
whether Powers would like to go to Moscow "without any
guards." Powers, too, assumed something odd was happening, but did not know what. Powers went to Moscow and
spent the night there. At no time did the Russians ever
mention Abel.

On Thursday, February 8, Donovan journeyed to East
Berlin again. This time the deal was sealed. Shishkin
flipped through a sheaf of papers and declared: "Everything has been approved by Moscow."

That evening Powers was on his way from Moscow to
Berlin.

In New York, two cars left the Henry Hudson Hotel at
2:15 P.M. and drove south to the detention headquarters.
The cars parked on Eleventh Street. After a moment a thin
man dressed all in brown, and wearing dark glasses, walked
up Eleventh Street with the jail's acting warden. The thin
man carried two canvas satchels. Wilkinson stepped out
onto the sidewalk.

Abel broke into a big grin as he recognized his old
warden. "I'm glad it's you," he told him. Then he asked

Wilkinson what was happening. The prison official said he could not guarantee anything, but it appeared that Abel might be repatriated.

"Do you want to go home?" Wilkinson asked the Soviet spy.

"Yes," Abel replied. "I'd like to see my wife and daughter. I'd like to go home." He did not say what country he meant.

Aldredge walked to the door of the jail and picked up a bundle containing handcuffs, guns, and ammunition. Abel stepped into the first car and sat in the rear with Aldredge on his left and Wilkinson on his right. A C.I.A. agent was in the front seat alongside the driver. Aldredge had stuffed the ammunition in his pockets in case Abel grabbed for the guns.

As the two cars moved along the waterfront, Abel commented: "I haven't been here in some time."

The car slid through the Holland Tunnel under the Hudson River, and Abel said, "I wonder where we're going."

"To tell you the truth," Wilkinson said, "I don't know either." As they drove on, Abel and his guards talked about the paintings he had left behind at Atlanta. The spy had a few suggestions on improving the American penal system.

Soon they arrived at Maguire Air Force Base, New Jersey. Abel, Aldredge, Wilkinson, and the C.I.A. man boarded a C-118 Constellation at 5:20 P.M. The plane took off forty minutes later. The crew did not know Abel's identity and was very curious, but the mysterious passengers offered no explanations.

The four men dined on steak over the Atlantic. Abel did not sleep. He read the New York papers and a paperback book about five hundred people selected to go underground because the world was about to be devastated by an atom bomb. The prison officials took turns sitting with Abel. They feared he perhaps really did not want to go back and face Moscow, and might try suicide.

As dawn broke, the four men whom circumstance had thrown together admired the sunrise. They moved their watches up six hours. At 6:30 A.M., local time, the plane landed in Wiesbaden to refuel. The pilot announced that the radio on the plane needed repairs. A curtain was strung completely around Abel, and only then was the repair man allowed on board. Another pilot also came aboard to guide the plane through the air corridor to Berlin.

As the plane droned over East Germany, Abel appeared to know exactly where he was. A MIG fighter rose and circled the plane but did not buzz it.

At 12:45 P.M. Friday, February 9, the plane landed at its destination—Tempelhof Airport, Berlin. Cars were waiting and "the package" was transported to a cell at Andrews Army Base, Berlin. Two guards were assigned, one or the other to keep Abel under observation at all times. All of the spy's clothes were taken away and he was given pajamas—after the strings had been removed from them. Abel asked for his shaving kit, but was handed an electric shaver instead.

The same day, Donovan went to East Berlin for one final meeting with Shishkin to work out last-minute details of the exchange. "I will meet you at 8:20 A.M.," Shishkin told him as the meeting ended, "at the Glienicker Bridge."

The seldom-used bridge was at the end of the Koenigstrasse, on the southwest edge of Berlin, a broad country road that ran to Potsdam. The span separated the American sector of West Berlin from East Germany.

Early Saturday morning, February 10, Donovan spent

a half-hour with Abel in his cell. He had, under the rules of American justice, fought hard for his client. Now the case was about to be marked closed.

Looking back on the scene later, Donovan recalled, "We discussed various matters, including the end of almost five years since the Bar Association got me into this. We were two dissimilar men drawn close by fate and the American law. From the start we had no differences. I called him 'Rudolf.' He called me 'Mr. Donovan.'"

At 6:45 A.M., Donovan, Lightner, and Wilkinson met in the Provost Marshal's office and studied the area around the Glienicker Bridge on a large wall map. Forty-five minutes later, they left, in two small German cars, with Abel in the second one. The prison officials were armed now for the first time. Abel appeared to know Berlin. He pointed out bombed ruins and said that war was a shameful thing to inflict on civilians.

The two cars stopped 150 yards from the bridge. Other cars were parked all around the area, out of sight. The East German police were watching the Americans with binoculars from their side of the bridge, although the mists interfered.

The two cars eased to within fifty yards of the bridge. Donovan, Lightner, and the C.I.A. man, who was called "Murphy," got out and began walking to the center of the bridge, at 8:20 A.M.

At a signal, the three moved forward with Abel. That appeared to excite Shishkin, who was already waiting in the center of the bridge. "Two, two, two!" he yelled.

But the group continued forward and now each camp stood facing the other across the white line. Donovan was in front, with "Murphy" behind him and to his left, and

Lightner to the right. Five yards further back, Abel stood manacled to Wilkinson.

Shishkin faced Donovan. "Cousin Drews" and an unidentified man stood just behind the Russian. Powers was five yards behind them, between two large men, wearing a fur hat, and a heavy coat over the blue trousers Barbara had sent to him in prison. He had four suitcases, including one filled with toys and souvenirs for his nieces and nephews.

At 8:30 A.M., "Cousin Drews" crossed the line and identified Abel. "Murphy," who once had served as a flier with Powers and knew him, crossed over and identified the U-2 pilot.

Wilkinson told Abel to take off his hat and dark glasses as "Cousin Drews" gazed at the Soviet spy. Abel obeyed and smiled as the other man identified him. The two men exchanged a few words of greeting in English.

At 8:35 A.M., Shishkin told Donovan that Frederic Pryor had been released at the Friedrichstrasse crossing. Standing in the chill morning air on the bridge, the two men chatted together during the awkward wait while Pryor's release was being confirmed by telephone.

"You should take a greater part in government activity," Shishkin advised Donovan, "and you should study Russian."

"In the United States," replied Donovan, "only the optimists study Russian. The pessimists study Chinese." Shishkin was not amused.

Behind Donovan, Wilkinson turned to Abel during the lull and asked, "Do you think your wife and daughter will be at the other end of the bridge?"

"No," said Abel, "I think they are in Leipzig."

At the white line, Shishkin was demanding "the document, the document." What he wanted was Kennedy's commutation order.

Finally, an American Army colonel returned to announce that Pryor had been released.

Wilkinson got down on one knee, and propping the paper on the other, he wrote: "Released Feb. 10, 1962. 8:52 A.M. Glienicker Bridge." After a brief argument between the Russians and the Americans over the spelling of the name of the bridge, Wilkinson handed the document to Abel.

Donovan watched Abel for the last time as he walked over the line and disappeared into the group of Soviet civilians.

The sun was just breaking through the mist over the Havel as Francis Gary Powers stepped across the six-inch white line.

17

A Summing Up

TWENTY-FOUR DAYS AFTER THE exchange on the bridge, Powers made his first public appearance, before the Senate Armed Services Committee. From the time he had set foot on American soil until he walked into the Senate Caucus Room on Capitol Hill, Powers had been hidden and interrogated by the C.I.A.[1]

At the public hearing, the U-2 pilot gave a lengthy version of his flight, capture and imprisonment, adding little to his testimony at the trial in Moscow.

"There was one thing that I always remembered

---

[1] Two hours before he testified, the C.I.A. issued a report which found he had fulfilled his contract and lived up to "his obligations as an American under the circumstances in which he found himself." It said he had volunteered for a lie detector test and had proved his truthfulness. It also said he would get his back pay.

while I was there," he said, "and that was that I am an
American."

The overflow audience applauded. The Senators
heaped praise upon him and refrained from asking searching questions. For example, no one inquired whether he
had been under a mandatory order to destroy the plane.

It was obvious from the C.I.A. report that the intelligence agency did not want any close scrutiny of the question. The report said the destructor unit was designed
merely to wreck the camera and equipment. But at the
same time, it indicated Powers hesitated at pushing the
destructor button for fear the whole plane would blow up
before he could get out.

"At this point," the report said, "he states he could
have reached the destruct switches which would have set
off an explosive charge in the bottom of the plane. However, he realized that this charge would go off in seventy
seconds and he did not yet know if he could leave the
plane."

Only the C.I.A. knows precisely what would have
happened had Powers pushed the button. Only Powers
knows all of the thoughts that passed through his mind
when he did not.

Exactly what brought Powers down remained a mystery. But the C.I.A. experts, according to Representative
Carl Vinson, Georgia Democrat who released the report,
concluded the U-2 was disabled at 68,000 feet by a near
miss from a ground-to-air missile.

Regardless of what had happened on May 1, 1960,
however, the 68,000-foot question was academic by 1962.
The best military judgment then was that Russian rockets
could, indeed, knock down a plane at that height.

This did not mean they had perfected an absolute

defense against the manned bomber, since all areas of the
Soviet Union were not protected by advanced antiaircraft
missiles. Also U. S. bombers had been equipped with air-
to-ground missiles which gave them the ability to launch
their warheads while flying outside the range of Russian
rockets.

But the really important questions of the U-2 affair
go beyond Francis Gary Powers and what happened to his
plane.

From the outset, the central mystery has been why
the plane was sent over the Soviet Union on May 1, 1960,
only fifteen days before the summit meeting. Was the
timing a coincidence?

A careful examination of all the available evidence
leads to the conclusion that it was not. The dispatch of the
plane was directly related to the summit.

Within the intelligence community of the United
States government, there was an uneasy feeling as the
summit approached that a *détente* might be reached at
Paris. If so, the U-2's might be grounded, perhaps per-
manently. An international rapprochement, followed by
Eisenhower's trip to Russia, would make further flights
politically impossible for the foreseeable future. As one
of those who managed the program put it: "We felt this
would literally be the last flight because of the summit."

There was a strong desire, therefore, to get one last
mission in under the wire. The policy-makers at the top of
the government were unable to resist this desire, since
they had already lost genuine control of the U-2 program.
Responsibility had been delegated for such a long time
that only the intelligence technicians were really able to
make a judgment on the value of each flight. They argued
that it was essential that certain targets be photographed

immediately. Such was the momentum of the program
that the Administration's leaders found it difficult to dis-
sent. And so the plane was sent, despite the fact that
there had been suspensions during sensitive periods in
the past.

There is no substantiated evidence of any sort of con-
spiracy to scuttle the summit. But it is clear that many
important persons in the intelligence field were more concerned with the U-2 as a valuable instrument of espionage
than with its possible effect on the summit. In other words,
they were worried not so much that the U-2 might endanger the summit as that the summit might endanger
the U-2. By May of 1960, intelligence had come to domi-
nate policy in the U-2 program. Instead of serving as a
basis for policy-making, intelligence-gathering had become an end in itself.

In a sense, the danger was inherent from the start.
The U-2 operation was a complete break with the traditional methods of espionage. And yet there is no evidence
that the revolutionary implications of the operation were
thought through. Eisenhower reluctantly accepted assurances that the Russians would not dare expose the program, but he apparently did not face up to the possibility
that there would be a day of reckoning.

There was a tendency on the part of both the policy-
makers and the intelligence men to avoid planning for the
worst. There was too much reliance on the technical means
of destroying the evidence and not enough awareness of
the chance of human or mechanical failure. Although
there was a cover story, it did not in fact cover all the
contingencies. When disaster struck, the government was
not ready, even though the program had been running for
four years. As a result, it stumbled into a series of errors.

The first, perhaps, was to issue any cover story at all. It might have been wiser to wait for the Russians to make the initial move and then to respond to each charge with the simple statement: "We are investigating."

Instead, on May 5, when Khrushchev disclosed that the plane had been downed, the government issued an elaborately detailed lie. That was the point of no return. When Khrushchev exposed the lie two days later, on May 7, the United States was confronted with the choice of admitting it had lied or of trying to brazen it out.

The government hedged by stating a half-truth—acknowledging the flight but insisting it had not been authorized by Washington.

But when the President realized the full implication of the statement, he felt the necessity of asserting his full responsibility for the program. When he did so, a new and crucial element was added—the indication that the flights were to continue. This was done despite the fact that Eisenhower knew, and said privately, that the flights were a blown instrument and would have to stop.

By lying, when it could have remained silent, by admitting it had lied, by disclaiming Presidential responsibility, then admitting Presidential responsibility, and finally by implying the flights would continue, the United States all but made it impossible for the summit meeting to take place.

It is difficult to see how any head of government could have been expected to sit down at a peace conference under the veiled public threat of further violations of his air space. To reverse the circumstances is to see the situation clearly: if, on the eve of a summit meeting, Khrushchev had threatened to send his planes over New York or Chicago, could Eisenhower—or any other president—have agreed to sit down with him?

It is true that Eisenhower finally announced at the summit table that he had called off the U-2 flights, but by then it was too late. It is quite possible, even probable, that Khrushchev came to Paris ready to blow up the summit. But this misses the point. By the time the summit convened on May 16, Washington had already taken a position—on May 9—that would have made it politically hazardous for Khrushchev to participate and still hope to remain Premier of the Soviet Union.

It would have been especially hazardous if, as is widely believed by experts on Soviet affairs, Khrushchev was then under strong pressure from the Chinese Communists and his own military. Khrushchev had staked his reputation on the premise that he could deal with Eisenhower. Now, to sit down with him was to run the risk of being condemned as a man who was soft on capitalism.

Exactly what was going on in the inner circle of the Kremlin is, of course, unknown. An interesting question is why Khrushchev chose to admit that a U-2 had penetrated 1,200 miles into Soviet territory. He could have said nothing, or he could have attempted to stop the flights through private overtures to Eisenhower.

A possible answer—as Eisenhower seemed to suspect from the start—is that Khrushchev realized that the only way he could be sure of stopping the flights was to protest publicly. At the same time he could then use the incident to place pressure on those nations which were providing overseas bases for the United States—a tender subject for the Soviets since the end of World War II.

The 1960 summit collapse is still too recent to be judged in proper historical perspective. However, it occurred at a time when East and West appeared to be moving slowly toward a *détente*. An atmosphere might have been created in which some specific problems could have been resolved, including, possibly, the first steps toward a ban on nuclear testing.

Instead, the cold war returned and Eisenhower's vision of peace was shattered. In retrospect, the President realized that the crisis had been badly handled. He admitted privately that the United States jumped too soon in issuing its May 5 statement.[2] And he conceded that the Administration had become overconfident in its conduct of the U-2 operation.

There was reason for this overconfidence. The U-2 program had operated without exposure for four years, providing the underpinning for some of the most important policies of the Eisenhower years. It had convinced the President, as he expressed it in his farewell address, that the celebrated "bomber gap" and "missile gap" were "fiction." It had also persuaded him that Soviet advances in space were not as spectacular as they seemed, and that the Russians, too, were secretly experiencing their share of failures.

But in the process, the U-2 may have acquired something of a mystical importance to the Administration. Although the plane did bring back some breathtaking information from the areas over which it flew, it could not blanket the Soviet Union.

It is not inconceivable that Soviet military might was concealed in the unphotographed areas. To base defense planning and strategy on the assumption that an enemy's

---

[2] Eisenhower, in fact, said so in a filmed interview with C.B.S. But this portion of the film was snipped out at the insistence of Lieutenant Colonel John Eisenhower, the President's son. It was not shown on the November 23, 1961, program, "C.B.S. Reports," in which the former President discussed the U-2.

weapons can be surely located would seem a risky enterprise. When and if the "spy in the sky" satellite is perfected, there will be the same temptation to attribute to it an omniscience in intelligence. And there will be the same temptation for an administration to dismiss its critics by referring to secret information it alone possesses.

The U-2 affair revealed the extraordinary extent to which information and activities that are secret to the American people are shaping the nation's destiny. Secrecy on a large scale became an accepted fact of life in the government's effort to survive in the postwar power struggle with Communism. As a result, a secret layer of government has developed spontaneously and established itself with the power to conceal its mistakes behind a claim of "national security." It includes, but is not limited to, the C.I.A. It has mushroomed to vast proportions outside the normal checks and balances of the government. It is largely ignored until its existence is exposed by a celebrated failure such as the U-2.

Beyond mere intelligence-gathering, the C.I.A. has engaged in subversion, the overthrow of unfriendly governments, attempted invasion, and other quasi-military operations. These activities may at times be necessary, but the extent to which they are consistent with our democratic institutions has never been properly assessed. Such a scrutiny would seem to be long overdue. Out of it might come tighter control by Congress and the Executive branch.

As the 1961 Cuban invasion showed, no President is invulnerable to the influence and power of these forces, and no party or administration has a franchise on competence or incompetence. A President must be alert not only to the machinations of the enemy but also to the parochial pleading within his own house. One of the lessons of the U-2 affair is that the President must preside. The critical decision on May 7, in which the United States admitted spying, was too significant to have been debated in the absence of the President. Similarly, the U-2 flights were too dangerous to have been conducted with such limited Presidential direction. Neither the President, the Secretary of State, nor the Secretary of Defense, for example, knew at the time that Powers was in the air over the Soviet Union.

Perhaps the most important lesson of the U-2 affair is that the American government can thrive only on the confidence of the people. The U-2 incident provoked a crisis in that confidence. When the government lied to the Soviet Union, it also misled its own citizens.

For years—up to, including (and even after) the U-2 flight—the press of the nation, and presumably much of the public, took the government's word as gospel. There seemed to be no general realization that there are times when the government may have to lie to protect an intelligence operation (and times when it may do so for domestic political motives).

But the public sophistication that might have been acquired through the U-2 episode was not. When the RB-47 was shot down two months later, all of the government's statements were generally accepted at face value.

Similarly, when Powers was freed, most of the press unquestioningly accepted as fact the officially leaked version of what the pilot told the C.I.A. in utmost secrecy. Not many seemed to realize that there might be a mutuality of interest between the C.I.A. and the Administration to redeem the public image of the intelligence agency through the Powers hearing.

At the time of the trial, Powers had come under considerable attack in the United States for seemingly having criticized his country. At the Senate hearing, he claimed that he acted on the advice of his defense counsel and that his apparent expressions of regret at the trial could be interpreted in another way.

". . . It was easy to say I was sorry because what I meant by saying that and what I wanted them to think I meant was quite different. My main sorrow was that the mission failed and I was sorry that I was there, and it was causing a lot of adverse publicity to the States."

Francis Gary Powers had never expected to become the most publicized spy in the cold war.

He flew the U-2 as a vocation, not as a dedication. But the work took courage, even if the rewards were ample. When his mission failed, many jumped to the conclusion that he was a disloyal American. There was an attempt to make him a scapegoat for all that happened, including the mistakes of the highest officials of the government. When he returned, the government led the effort to banish the unpleasant memory of the U-2 affair from the national conscience by casting him in the role of a hero.

The truth is that he was neither. He was an ordinary man sent out on an extraordinary mission.

Authors' Note

THIS BOOK WAS WRITTEN without the official cooperation of any agency or individual in the government and over the active opposition of some. Nevertheless, the authors have voluntarily omitted certain information, particularly dealing with current intelligence operations, in the belief that the national interest would best be served by withholding it.

During a year of research, the authors conducted hundreds of hours of interviews and talked to more than a hundred persons, including virtually all of the officials and former officials of the United States government who took part in the decision-making before and after the flight of Francis Gary Powers over the Soviet Union on May 1, 1960.

They traveled some 15,000 miles, following leads and checking stories in the United States and overseas. The trail led all the way from a farmhouse on a dirt road near Pound, Virginia—Powers' home—to a villa in the Swiss-Italian Alps.

The authors were in the cockpit of a U-2 and interviewed several U-2 pilots. They sat in Oliver Powers' shoe repair shop in Norton, Virginia, and in the glittering room at the Elysée Palace in Paris where the 1960 summit conference collapsed. They interviewed five of the men who were inside the room that day.

They visited the Lockheed Aircraft Corporation plant at Burbank, California, where the U-2 was built. And they talked at length with three of Powers' sisters, his mother, his father, several college classmates, and numerous friends.

The authors would like to express appreciation to all their colleagues who offered valuable assistance. The list presented here is not meant to be complete but it would have to include Julius Frandsen, Jr., of United Press International, and John Brady of the UPI mechanical department; Charles Roberts, Lloyd H. Norman, Henry T. Simmons, Osborn Elliott, and Edward Weintal, of *Newsweek* (which granted us permission to reproduce some of the letters in Chapter 15); Lucy Jarvis, Al Wasserman, Walter Millis, Jr., and especially Penny Bernstein, of the N.B.C. White Paper staff which produced the excellent documentary on the U-2; Robert B. Hotz and Larry L. Booda, of *Aviation Week; Marvin Miles,* of the *Los Angeles Times;* Bill Hendrick, of the Coalfield (Va.) *Progress;* Douglas Kiker, of the *Atlanta Journal;* Roscoe Drummond; and Walter Lippmann.

Vero Roberti, of *Corriere della Sera;* Tom Lambert, of the *New York Herald Tribune;* Max Frankel, of the *New York Times,* and his wife, Tobia Frankel, gave invaluable advice on Moscow scenes. William A. Wise, the brother of one of the authors, was of considerable help in research problems.

Jean Chauveau, press secretary to President de Gaulle, was kind enough to allow us to go through the Elysée and study the room where the summit conference failed. We are grateful also to David Miller, Ralph Chapman and Robert Grayson, of the *New York Herald Tribune;* and particularly to Robert J. Donovan, chief of the paper's Washington bureau, and to Carleton V. Kent, Jr., Washington bureau chief of the *Chicago Sun-Times,* for their advice and encouragement.

The authors are principally indebted to many persons who cannot be mentioned. Normally, a reader expects the sources of material in a book to be identified, but this presents a problem in a work of current history. This book could not have been written without the help of many individuals still serving in the government or active in public life. They were willing to be interviewed, often at some personal risk, because they saw a larger national interest in presenting the facts.

To these men and women this book is truly dedicated.

Index

271